How to Interpret Data

Creating Success books are available at
www.koganpage.com/creating-success
and booksellers worldwide

THE **CREATING SUCCESS** SERIES
Over 1.8 million copies sold

How to Deal with Difficult People by Roy Lilley
How to Improve Your Communication Skills by Alan Barker
How to Interpret Data by Nicholas Kelly
How to Manage People by Michael Armstrong
How to Manage Projects by Paul J Fielding
How to Manage Remotely by Gemma Dale
How to Negotiate by Mike Clayton
How to Write a Business Plan by Brian Finch
How to Write a Marketing Plan by John Westwood

ABOUT THE AUTHOR

Nicholas Kelly is a principal at G&K Consulting. He is a leader in analytics adoption, having designed dashboards for some of the world's largest companies, from global banks to Formula 1 teams. A frequent speaker at international conferences, he has trained thousands of professionals in data visualization and analytics adoption. He is the author of *Delivering Data Analytics*, also published by Kogan Page.

How to Interpret Data

Using data to improve your influence and decision-making

Nicholas Kelly

KoganPage

First published in Great Britain and the United States in 2025 by Kogan Page Limited

Kogan Page

Kogan Page Ltd, 2nd Floor, 45 Gee Street, London EC1V 3RS, United Kingdom
Kogan Page Inc, 8 W 38th Street, Suite 902, New York, NY 10018, USA
www.koganpage.com

EU Representative (GPSR)

Authorised Rep Compliance Ltd, Ground Floor, 71 Baggot Street Lower, Dublin D02 P593, Ireland
www.arccompliance.com

Kogan Page books are printed on paper from sustainable forests.

ISBNs

Hardback   978 1 3986 1988 3
Paperback   978 1 3986 1974 6
Ebook   978 1 3986 1987 6

British Library Cataloguing-in-Publication Data

A CIP record for this book is available from the British Library.

Library of Congress Control Number

2025934288

Typeset by Hong Kong FIVE Workshop
Print production managed by Jellyfish
Printed and bound by CPI Group (UK) Ltd, Croydon CR0 4YY

CONTENTS

This book is dedicated to my wife, Maria, my unwavering partner, whose boundless love for our children and relentless pursuit of excellence are an inspiration. Your attention to detail and dedication in every facet of life form the foundation on which our family grows and thrives. You are the heart of our journey, driving us toward greatness together.

To Aiden, the forger of paths. Your curious mind, ever seeking to unravel the mysteries of the universe, and your unyielding determination to overcome any challenge will lead you to remarkable heights. Never lose that spark, it is your gift to the world. You lead by example. Thank you for being a conscientious and thoughtful son.

To Athena, a challenger of assumptions and a leader in thought and action. Your creativity, clarity and ability to get to the heart of every matter are truly unique, as well as your sense of humour. Your fearless spirit and vision are shaping a future only you can imagine. Thank you for all the joy you bring and for being our special girl.

To our family, the greatest blessing of my life. Each of you brings a light that illuminates our journey, and together we navigate with love, joy and purpose.

PREFACE

When my publisher asked me to write this book, I was in the middle of a very large consulting project for a client and scarcely had the time to reply. Not to mention the chaos of family life. My immediate thought went to how hard it was to write my first book and whether I wanted to put myself and my family through that again.

However, there were two factors that influenced my decision to write it. Firstly, our kids were getting to the age where they were becoming curious about what our data consulting business was all about. Indeed, I was already playing with the idea of volunteering to teach an extracurricular class on how to analyse data at their elementary school. I thought this would be a fun way for them to explore the topic with their friends. However, that would necessitate me creating a curriculum for complete beginners to the topic. So that was simmering in the back of my mind.

Secondly, with our clients, a consistent trend over the years was the knowledge gap some stakeholders had in what data is and how to work with it. Some of the greatest points of friction were from stakeholders expecting data work to be trivial and easy to do. You might find yourself nodding your head at this point. Expectation, as I have learned the hard way, is the cause of many a failed analytics effort. So, at some point, I placed a to-do note on my office whiteboard to create a guide for newcomers to data to help them understand the effort and work involved in working with data.

With the above context in mind, writing the book on *How to Interpret Data* made sense. Obviously, it is a very large topic to tackle in a concise way. Determining what to include and how to include it became the biggest challenge in attempting to distill very complex ideas into a relatively short format. When determining what to include in this book, I drew on my over 20 years of consulting experience. For instance, I included a section on averages because they are often misunderstood, while I chose not to delve deeply into regression analysis and predictive models. My guiding principle has been straightforward: if a lack of understanding on a topic frequently hinders the adoption and use of data for decision-making, it has earned a place in these pages.

I want this book to be something I can hand to a client, friend or anyone interested in learning more about how to use data and what it entails. So, it is written with the assumption that the reader is mid-career in business, but a newcomer to data. Reading this book will equip the data novice with a deeper understanding of what it takes to work with data and use it for decision-making.

I hope you enjoy it and thank you for taking the time to read it!

HOW TO USE THIS BOOK

As mentioned, data interpretation is a vast and multifaceted topic, encompassing concepts, techniques and practical applications that touch on every aspect of decision-making. This book serves as your guide to navigating that complexity, but no single resource can cover every detail. That's why this book is paired with a companion website. The website expands on the content here, offering additional examples, charts and more detailed datasets to work with. Indeed, it is intended that you leverage the website to download and directly work through some of the examples that are introduced in the book.

The website has a list of recommended tools you can use for working through exercises and how you can get access to them. In general, the tools are free (Power BI) or are included in existing subscriptions that you might already have (e.g. Excel).

The end of each chapter includes an example that builds on the concepts being discussed, as well as exercises designed to help you apply what you've learned. While you're encouraged to follow the book sequentially, it's not a requirement. Feel free to jump between chapters as your interests or needs dictate. The structure allows you to explore specific areas without needing to master everything at once.

It's also worth noting that you may not need to know every aspect of the processes outlined here or even be the one implementing each step. However, working through the exercises, even for tasks outside your typical role, will deepen your understanding of what each step entails. This insight will not only make you a more effective collaborator but also give you a clearer sense of the bigger picture.

Whether you're just starting your journey with data or seeking to refine your skills, this book is a practical tool designed to grow with you. Use it as a reference, a workbook and a source of inspiration for how data can drive meaningful decisions.

Companion website: www.howtointerpretdata.com

Part 1
The foundations of data interpretation

01
Why data matters to your career

Imagine you are the captain of an ancient ship, steering it in a stormy sea. The waves are crashing, sailors are falling overboard, the winds are shifting and your compass is broken. You are desperate to reach the shore, but without direction, every decision feels like a gamble. The hull is violently creaking under the strain of the ferocious tide. Every moment, you're faced with critical decisions: do you unfurl the sails to harness the wind and move faster to potential land, knowing you might rip them to shreds and leave the ship vulnerable? Or do you keep them furled, moving slowly but safely, even though the storm is closing in and land is nowhere in sight?

For decades, businesses operated this way. Leaders and managers relied on intuition and experience, making decisions without concrete data to guide them. Sometimes they navigated successfully, but often they crashed into unseen rocks, derailed by shifting consumer demands and market changes they couldn't anticipate.

But today, the modern business depends on data. Data has become the compass that helps business leaders and managers navigate the chaotic and undulating tides of commerce. Businesses no longer need to guess. They can see where their customers are going, what they want and where the next opportunity, or danger, lies. Data isn't just a tool; it's the lifeline keeping companies afloat and even, for those willing to invest in data, making them stand out from their competitors.

Data is everywhere, but it does not magically transform into useful and actionable information. It needs to be interpreted, communicated and actioned. While many companies claim to have collected vast amounts of data for their business, few have adapted themselves to fully extract all the value it offers. Those who do not have a path to unlock that value risk languishing in the ocean of failure. Just ask Blockbuster, the once-dominant video rental chain that failed to see the rise of digital streaming as its greatest threat. While Netflix embraced data to shape its business model, tracking viewer behaviour, identifying trends and creating personalized experiences, Blockbuster remained anchored in the past. By the time they tried to catch up, it was too late. Netflix thrived while Blockbuster sank beneath the waves.

Or take Kodak, the photography giant that failed to evolve. Even though they saw the digital revolution coming, they missed the data signals flashing before them. While consumer preferences shifted from film to digital, Kodak clung to its legacy business, which it had years and years of highly successful experience in, refusing to adapt. By the time it embraced the inevitable, it had lost the very market it had been instrumental in creating.

These are not just cautionary tales of big brands but lessons in what happens when companies ignore data. Businesses, like living organisms, need feedback to survive. They must adapt to changing environments, sense new opportunities and move quickly when storms are on the horizon. Those that don't? They face extinction.

That brings us to you and the reason you are reading this book. You have probably noticed that the term 'data' is often thrown around. But you have probably also noticed that it might not impact as much as the hype suggests. Why is that, you ask?

If anything, it is as much about the data as it is about the people interpreting it and how successfully they influence others to act on it. In the above examples of Blockbuster and Kodak, it is not like there was a dearth of data. Some people saw it. Indeed, people in each of those organizations saw it. So, if the data existed, and some people knew about it, why did the businesses not correct their course? Because the right people, who could course correct, were not influenced by either the data or the people who saw the data.

If you want to understand data, you must also know how to influence others to act on that data. Data without action is like having a map but not using it to navigate. Many can understand data, and this book will help you with that, but few and far between are those who have the tools to make that data have an impact. This book will also help you to bridge that gap.

A lesson from Netflix

The story of Netflix's early use of data for strategic business decisions is fascinating and began well before the streaming giant shifted to creating its own content. Netflix, at its core, leverages data in every major strategic decision. Early on, Netflix recognized that its business model, renting DVDs by mail, needed continuous evolution to stay competitive, and it leveraged data to adapt to its environment and gather feedback on the impact of those decisions.

Netflix analysed customer behaviour, including when users would return DVDs, how long they kept them and what kinds of movie preferences they had, like action movies or thrillers. This data-driven approach allowed them to introduce personalized recommendations based on rental history, which kept customers engaged and coming back for more. By associating what other customers rented, they could recommend what customers who liked the same movies might want. It is one of the very early examples of a data-driven recommendation engine. Not only were customers able to rent what they liked, but they were also getting curated recommendations from the convenience of their homes, which Blockbuster could not match.

Not ones to sit on their heels, based on how they interpreted the data they were collecting, Netflix also upended the industry-standard payment model for customers from a per-rental model to a subscription-based service. This was obviously a significant strategic decision but one that paid off. They tracked how frequently customers rented movies and used this information to create subscription plans that aligned with customer behaviour, allowing for unlimited rentals without the stress of late fees. This pivot put them ahead of Blockbuster, which was slower to adapt and still reliant on brick-and-mortar locations with the burden of their associated costs.

An important moment came when Netflix invested in the future and the rise of streaming. In the early 2000s, internet speeds were still slow, but by the mid-2000s, trends indicated that internet speeds and bandwidth were increasing to the point that streaming movies might be feasible. In addition, consumer behaviour was leaning towards instant, on-demand access without the hassle of needing to post movies back. Instead of clinging to their DVD business, Netflix went all in on streaming. Their understanding of shifting customer expectations underpinned this decision. While Blockbuster hesitated, Netflix was already using data to develop and refine its streaming service, allowing it to dominate the space and secure a significant and insurmountable foothold.

These data-led decisions marked the early days and rapid rise of Netflix. But, while those strategic decisions made a large impact in an obvious way, perhaps less obvious is how it used, and uses, data to create content. Through its online streaming service, Netflix was able to collect vast amounts of data on viewer preferences, behaviours and viewing patterns. Having this data was not what drove continued success; it was Netflix's ability to interpret the data that made it the leader it is today.

By analysing viewer data, Netflix could predict what content would resonate with different audiences. This data-driven decision led to it creating the hit show *House of Cards*. The data revealed that a large segment of viewers enjoyed films directed by David Fincher and those starring Kevin Spacey. At the same time, the political drama genre was on an upward trend in popularity. Bringing all these elements together, Netflix confidently invested millions into the show's production without needing a pilot episode, knowing with certainty it would get a substantial return on investment.

As we now know, the show was a great success, and it marked a shift in how Netflix leveraged data not just for content delivery but for content creation, moving them to even greater heights within the industry.

This is what good data interpretation can do: it moves beyond the numbers and informs strategic, operational and tactical decisions that produce tangible results. Without skilfully interpreting viewer data, Netflix may have missed this opportunity to reshape the entertainment industry. However, it was not just the interpretation of those numbers; it was having the structure and will to act on that data.

The recipe for success

Netflix is just one example, albeit an obvious and relatable one. Yet many more help illustrate how data is used to support decision-making across all industries and can suggest how you might be able to learn from these examples and apply them to your situation.

In healthcare, a company called Truemed, based in Texas, is using a data-driven approach to improve people's health by focusing on illness prevention through diet, exercise, supplements and other environmental changes. Like Netflix, Truemed uses a personalized approach but bases its recommendations on lab results such as blood tests. They can then identify common markers for health and illness and, where possible, target lifestyle causes of those issues. From this, they can create customized plans for optimal health, including nutrition, supplements and lifestyle interventions designed to target specific deficiencies and health risks. These plans are highly actionable, but of course, it is up to each person to action those recommendations and make the necessary changes to their lives. Indeed, the suggested changes are often the hardest part of working with data – a theme we will see keeps repeating itself.

We are all familiar with Amazon and how personalized the shopping experience is based on a sophisticated recommendation engine that analyses customer buying behaviour, purchases and browsing history. With this data, Amazon can predict what customers will likely buy next and what offers would convert them to a purchase. Every suggestion on your screen, from product recommendations to the 'Customers who bought this also bought' section, results from data being leveraged in the background. While it may seem commonplace now, data is at the very foundation of Amazon's success.

Yet, in its wake, is a battlefield of companies that failed to leverage data. Retailers like Sears and Toys 'R' Us, for example, once dominated their sectors but were slow to adopt data-driven strategies. They relied too heavily on brick-and-mortar sales, missing out on the power of online retail and the deep customer analysis that comes with the market channel. As a result, they struggled to compete with Amazon's personalized, data-backed shopping experience.

You are probably noticing a pattern here. Both Netflix and Amazon took advantage of a changing world and used data to help them navigate uncertainty. However, which came first – the changes in their environment or having access to data naturally leading to a more optimal level of service and customer experience?

When data contradicts intuition

Michael Burry, the hedge fund manager made famous by the movie *The Big Short* for predicting the 2008 financial crisis, is a prime example of how data can lead to incredibly contrarian decisions while under extreme pressure to go with the consensus view with very large sums of money at stake. Indeed, it is a prime example of following what the data is telling you while under pressure.

In the early 2000s, Burry noticed something deeply troubling in the US housing market. Most investors thought buying property was a safe bet and that house prices would always rise. But Burry, through careful analysis of data on subprime mortgages, saw a different story unfolding. Digging into the numbers, he noticed that many mortgages were being given to high-risk individuals who were unlikely to be able to meet their repayment obligations. He realized that a significant portion of these subprime loans would ultimately default, leading to the collapse of the market because there were so many of them. Most other investors were either ignoring this or were oblivious to it.

What set Burry apart was his ability to interpret the data and connect the dots that others couldn't or wouldn't see. He analysed mortgage-backed securities tied to these loans and predicted their value would plummet when people defaulted. Despite the continued optimism of the housing market, Burry acted based on his data analysis.

One unpopular move was his decision to create and invest in credit default swaps (CDS), financial instruments that would allow him to bet against these subprime bonds. He was basically taking out insurance on something he thought would fail, i.e. the housing market. His analysis showed that the risk was underpriced, so he bought a substantial number of these swaps. The thing is, it wasn't just his money; he was buying on behalf of his clients, some of whom did not agree with him.

While the housing market continued to rise, Burry faced immense pressure from these clients. His peers questioned his strategy. Many thought he was nuts for betting against what was widely considered one of the safest investments at the time, but Burry stuck to his data-backed convictions. He could see that the housing market was a ticking time bomb.

Well, as we know, the housing bubble burst in 2007, and Burry's bet on data paid off. The default swaps skyrocketed in value, earning him and his investors hundreds of millions of dollars in profits while the rest of the market tanked.

The most remarkable part of Burry's story wasn't his ability to spot the collapse, though that was impressive; it was his persistence in relying on data even when everyone else disagreed. While others went with the consensus or herd mentality, Burry focused on what the numbers told him. He exemplified the power of data interpretation: not simply looking at the data but also understanding its implications deeply enough to make bold, decisive moves that others were unwilling to make.

Your role in data interpretation

Whether you are hesitant to work with data or not, an important step is to recognize your critical role in interpreting it. As we saw in the Michael Burry example, it is not just about the numbers; it is about translating those numbers into stories, insights, and actions that people can relate to and that can drive you and your organization forward.

Indeed, regardless of your specific role, whether you are a manager, entrepreneur or executive, you are the bridge between the data and the decisions it forms. You don't need to be a data scientist to understand the basics of data interpretation. Being actively involved in the interpretation process ensures you align the data insights with your business's unique challenges, objectives and needs.

As we will see later, data doesn't exist in a vacuum. The context in which data is generated plays a significant role in how it should be interpreted. You know your business, your industry and your customers/stakeholders. This knowledge gives you an upper hand in making sense of the numbers. For example, sales might drop one month and go up in another, but without the context of seasonality, market changes or a recent market push, those numbers alone would not provide meaningful insights.

By taking an active role in the interpretation process, you can ensure that data is being applied in the right context and that time is not being wasted. You'll be able to flag when something doesn't seem right or cannot be easily explained through your understanding of the business.

While your role with data is important, it doesn't mean you need or should work in isolation. Collaborating with data professionals like analysts, data scientists or IT professionals can give you a deeper and clearer picture. Your understanding of the business, combined with their technical skill, creates a powerful combination. Together, you can ensure that data is collected and effectively analysed, interpreted and acted upon to impact business goals.

Overcoming data anxiety

For many of us, the world of data can initially feel overwhelming or intimidating. You might wonder, 'Where do I start?' or 'What if I get it wrong?' Understandably, this fear can stop people from engaging with data at all, leading to missed opportunities and possible lack of career advancement.

The first step to overcoming data anxiety is recognizing that interpreting data is a skill that can be developed. It is not necessary to have all the answers from the outset, but you do need to take that first step. Begin by familiarizing yourself with the data relevant to your role and industry. Read about examples, like the Netflix one above, to get a deeper appreciation for the impact data can have in your field. Start small: pick a single dataset or report and focus on understanding what it tells you and what it means. You don't need to be Michael Burry to get started.

It can help to reframe how you approach data. Rather than being intimidated by it, view it as a powerful tool that can help you be more successful. Everyone makes mistakes with data at some point. The key is learning from those mistakes and refining your approach over time. The real mistake would be to never start down this path in the first place.

Building confidence with data is akin to learning a new language. The more you practise, the more fluent you become. Huge strides can be made with some straightforward data, and not every valuable insight requires the resources of Netflix or a team of data scientists. Often, the most beneficial impacts come from someone first asking the right question. As you will see, understanding data is but a part of the puzzle. Maybe that is a skill you currently lack, but your other qualities may come to the fore, such as having a curious mind and being able to communicate and influence.

By following the approach in this book, you will be able to build your confidence and will become more comfortable with data.

Starting small

Even some of the world's most successful business leaders started with basic, foundational data skills. Jeff Bezos didn't start his career as a data scientist, but his focus on customer data and patterns allowed Amazon to evolve into the data-powered giant it is today. Similarly, Reed Hastings, the founder of Netflix, didn't come from a background in statistics, but his reliance on customer viewing data transformed Netflix into a global media powerhouse.

They started small, looking at simple metrics, asking basic questions and slowly building their confidence in making decisions based on numbers. You can follow a similar path.

Here's where you can start:

- Ask the right questions: Before you even look at any data, get clear on the problem you're trying to solve or the question you want answered. For example, 'Why is customer engagement dropping?' or 'Which products are most popular among our top customers?'

- Identify patterns: Once you have the data, don't focus on every tiny detail. Instead, start looking for patterns or trends. Are certain products being purchased more frequently? Are customers abandoning their baskets after a certain point in the online checkout process?

- Use simple tools: Start with basic tools like Excel or Google Sheets. These are accessible, user-friendly and can help you manipulate data, build simple charts and extract insights. No need to dive into advanced software like Tableau or Power BI right away.

Even the most data-savvy professionals started with basic steps. The key is to embrace the learning process. It's easy to feel overwhelmed when you look at complex reports or dashboards, but remember that you don't need to understand every number or technical term to start making better decisions. Interpretation is about making sense of trends and patterns in the context of your business, not about performing complex statistical analysis.

Example

Throughout this book, you'll step into the role of a data analyst working as part of an HR analytics team in a mid-sized company. Your mission is to use data to address real-world business challenges and make meaningful recommendations that drive impactful decisions.

Your team's primary focus is on understanding employee engagement, improving retention and identifying opportunities for growth within the company. Over the coming chapters, you'll be guided through specific scenarios and challenges, each designed to help you build your data interpretation skills while learning how to influence actions based on insights.

For example, you might be tasked with identifying which employees are most at risk of leaving the company, uncovering drivers behind low engagement scores or proposing strategies to boost collaboration across teams. Along the way, you'll analyse employee metrics like training hours, internal communication patterns and supervisor performance ratings, applying structured frameworks to uncover actionable insights.

As you progress, you'll not only explore how to work with data but also practise crafting compelling stories that align your findings with business goals, ensuring your insights are understood and acted upon by decision-makers. This hands-on, step-by-step approach will prepare you to confidently interpret data and influence decisions in your own professional environment.

Let's get started by laying the foundation for what it means to think like a data-driven professional and why your role as a bridge between data and action is so critical.

Exercise

Now it's your turn to think like a data-driven leader. Imagine you're tasked with identifying the factors that contribute to employee engagement in your company. Your goal is to choose a few key metrics that will help you uncover actionable insights.

You've been provided with a table of potential metrics. However, since resources are limited, you can only analyse five metrics to start. Use the list below and select the ones you believe are most likely to impact employee engagement based on what you've learned so far.

Table 1.1 Employee metrics

Metric	Description
1. Commute distance	How far employees travel to work.
2. Salary growth rate	The rate at which an employee's salary has increased.
3. Supervisor performance	Employee satisfaction with their direct supervisor.
4. Number of sick days	Total sick days taken over the past year.
5. Internal communication	Frequency of participation in company-wide meetings or updates.
6. Cross-departmental projects	Number of collaborative projects involving multiple departments.
7. Training hours	Number of hours of training completed by the employee.

Table 1.1   *cont'd*

Metric	Description
8. Employee engagement survey results	Scores from recent engagement surveys.
9. Recognition programmes	Frequency of employees receiving recognition or awards.
10. Peer feedback	Feedback from peers and colleagues.

Questions to consider

1 Which metrics align most closely with what you think drives engagement in your company?
2 How might these metrics reveal patterns or trends that point to areas for improvement?
3 What actions could you take if the data showed concerning results for one or more of these metrics?

After making your selections, reflect on why you chose those metrics. Then, consider this hypothetical scenario: you notice that employees who participate in cross-departmental projects and receive regular peer feedback report higher engagement scores. How could you use this insight to influence company policies or programmes?

Summary points

● **Data matters for everyone**
  Data isn't just for analysts or tech experts. It's a strategic tool that helps professionals at all levels make informed, impactful decisions.

- **Data + action = value**
  Having data is not enough; you need to interpret it meaningfully and influence others to act on it. Insights that don't inspire change remain unrealized potential.

- **Confidence through understanding**
  Overcoming data anxiety starts with understanding what the data represents and how it can guide better decisions. Start small, ask clear questions and build your confidence step by step.

- **The human element is key**
  Successful data interpretation isn't purely technical. It requires understanding people – your stakeholders, your customers, your colleagues – and how they react to insights and recommendations.

- **A holistic view**
  Recognize that data interpretation is a journey. It begins by clarifying your goals and ends with influencing decisions that drive measurable outcomes. Each step, from defining what you need to communicating the final insight, adds value.

02
From data acquisition to influence

The data interpretation journey

When you think of working with data, it might seem like an obvious process: look at some numbers, draw conclusions and make decisions. It can be that if all the stars align. But, as you've probably experienced countless times, life is rarely smooth sailing. Like so many things, success with data isn't just about the moment of analysis; it's about preparation, execution and follow-through.

Think of a professional golfer's swing. The moment the club strikes the ball seems like the key action, but everything around it – the preparation, the stance, the motion and the follow-through – determines how far the ball travels and whether it reaches its target. Without a strong follow-through, even the best swing will fall short.

The journey begins long before analysis, defining what data to collect and why, and it doesn't stop at interpretation. The insights you uncover must carry into communication and influencing decisions, ensuring they lead to real action and measurable outcomes. Skipping steps or failing to follow through can result in wasted effort, missed opportunities and decisions that fail to deliver value.

In this chapter we introduce the five key steps of the data interpretation journey that form the basis for this book:

1 **Defining data needs:** Identifying the questions that need answering and aligning data to business goals.

2 **Data acquisition:** Collecting the right data from relevant sources.

3 **Data preparation:** Cleaning and organizing the data to ensure quality and usability.

4 **Data analysis:** Discovering patterns, trends and insights to inform decisions.

5 **Communication and influencing decisions:** Sharing findings effectively to drive action and impact.

You won't always need to follow every step in detail. Some projects may require quick analysis, while others demand meticulous preparation and deeper exploration. Over time, tools and automation can streamline parts of the process. However, understanding each stage and its purpose provides the foundation to work with data in any business setting effectively.

Like a golfer's swing, the preparation and follow-through make the difference. Let's begin with the first step: defining data needs, where all successful data interpretation starts.

Step 1: Defining data needs

Before you analyse any data, you need to ask a crucial question: *What data do I need, and why?* This step sets the foundation for the entire process. Without a clear understanding of your goals and the questions you need answered, it's easy to get lost in irrelevant details, collecting data that provides little value.

Defining data needs is about aligning your work with a purpose. You're not looking at data for its own sake; you're using it to solve problems, answer questions or make decisions that matter to your business. When you know what you're aiming for, you can be focused and intentional in collecting and using data.

Every project begins with a goal. What problem are you solving, or what opportunity are you trying to seize? Clear goals set the direction for everything that follows.

For example, if a company is struggling with high employee turnover, the goal might be 'Understand why employees are leaving and identify actions to improve retention.'

With a clear goal in mind, break it down into questions that data can answer. Well-crafted questions sharpen your focus and guide you to the right metrics. For example, 'Which departments have the highest turnover rates?' or 'How do training opportunities or promotions affect retention?'

Each question serves as a lens, helping you decide what data is worth collecting and analysing, whereas metrics bridge the gap between questions and answers. Metrics are the specific data points that help you measure what's happening. Important metrics that measure progress toward goals are called Key Performance Indicators (KPIs). For our turnover example, relevant metrics might include supervisor performance scores, employee engagement scores, training hours and number of promotions.

Sometimes, existing metrics may not perfectly answer your question. In those cases, you may need to get creative, identifying proxies and alternative measures that approximate the answer or defining new metrics to fit the purpose.

Once you know what you're looking for, the next step is figuring out where to get it. Data can come from many places, such as internal HR systems, performance reviews, employee surveys or even third-party sources. The ideal situation is that the data already exists and is accessible. You may need to collect it or find alternatives if it isn't. For example, employee engagement scores might come from internal surveys and promotion history and tenure could be found in HR records. The goal is to focus on the data that will help you answer your questions efficiently.

Defining your goals and needs ensures you don't waste time or resources. It helps you focus on collecting the right data so that every decision is grounded in purpose. Skipping this step is like trying to play golf blindfolded – you might take a swing but you won't know where the ball is going.

The clarity you gain here will carry through to every other step in the journey. When you know your goals, questions, metrics and data sources, you can move to the next stage of what data you need to answer these questions.

Step 2: Data acquisition

Not to diminish the importance of defining your data needs, but that can be easy compared to actually getting your hands on that data. At its best, this process is smooth: the data exists, it's well organized and you have the permissions and tools to access it. In a mature organization, this might mean pulling datasets from a centralized catalogue, where everything is neatly labelled, validated and ready to use.

However, in many organizations, this ideal setup is more aspiration than reality. The data landscape can feel scattered and fragmented, like playing a round of golf where you're searching for your ball in the rough. Ownership disputes, siloed systems and fragmented datasets can slow progress, turning what should be a simple step into a test of persistence and problem solving.

To stay on target, focus on the source of your data. Broadly, there are three key categories to consider: internal, external and new data. Internal is data generated within the organization, such as HR records, customer transactions, financial reports and operational metrics. External data includes information from outside the organization, including market research reports, government statistics, industry benchmarks or data from third-party providers. Finally, when existing data doesn't cut it, you may need to gather new information through methods like employee surveys, customer interviews, IoT sensors or feedback tools.

For example, if you're exploring employee turnover, you might pull HR records (internal data), reference industry benchmarks for turnover rates (external data) and design an engagement survey to gather employee sentiment (new data).

Acquiring data is rarely without obstacles. The process can feel more like navigating a tricky bunker shot in less mature environments than a smooth fairway. A typical issue is that different teams or departments hold data in isolated systems, making it difficult to access or integrate. Overcoming these data silos often requires building relationships and negotiating with data owners. Data privacy and ethics play a role with sensitive data, like HR records or customer information, which may require strict permissions to access. Understanding governance and privacy policies might seem like a barrier but such steps are necessary for trust and security.

Navigating these hurdles requires initiative, persistence and collaboration. Approach data owners with clarity, whether IT teams, HR managers or external partners, and explain what you're trying to achieve, why you need the data and how it aligns with the organization's goals. When people see the value of your work, they're far more likely to help you get what you need.

Acquiring the right data is like setting up for a perfect golf swing. If you start with poor alignment or faulty footing, everything that follows, including preparation, analysis and communication, will falter. Clean, targeted and reliable data gives you the confidence to move forward, much like a strong setup leads to a smooth follow-through.

By approaching data acquisition with structure and purpose, you lay the foundation for success. With your data in hand, you're ready for the next step: preparing it for analysis.

Step 3: Data preparation

This is probably the step you might be the least familiar with. This is where raw data transforms into something usable, clean and reliable. It's the equivalent of a golfer carefully setting up their stance, checking their grip and adjusting their alignment before taking the swing. Without this preparation, even the best data analysis will miss its mark.

The saying 'garbage in, garbage out' applies here: if your data is flawed, incomplete or inconsistent, any insights you derive will be unreliable and possibly misleading. A well-prepared dataset, however, gives you a solid foundation for uncovering patterns and trends that drive smart decisions.

At its core, this step focuses on two main activities: cleaning the data and combining it into a cohesive whole.

Data often arrives in a less-than-perfect state. Errors, inconsistencies and gaps can muddy the waters and impact the accuracy of your analysis. Cleaning involves filling in gaps where data is incomplete or deciding how to exclude them without skewing results. This includes fixing typos, duplicate entries and inconsistencies (e.g. 'New York' vs. 'NY') and ensuring consistent units, dates and naming conventions across datasets.

If you're working with multiple datasets, it may be necessary to connect them into a single, cohesive structure. This will require joining the data together across shared identifiers (e.g. employee IDs, customer numbers). We will explore the various joining approaches later in the book.

Data preparation can sometimes feel like smoothing out a tricky patch of grass on the fairway: it takes patience and attention to detail. Ensuring the quality of your data is paramount to being able to get accurate insights from it. Skipping or rushing through data preparation is like ignoring your setup before a golf swing: your analysis will go off target, no matter how good your technique is. Properly cleaned and combined data sets the stage for accurate, trustworthy insights and smooth analysis in the next step.

Step 4: Data analysis

Now it's time for the fun stuff! Indeed, you might have thought this would be the whole topic for the book. However, neglect of the preceding steps is why most analysis fails to move the needle. Analysis is when you start uncovering patterns, identifying trends and making sense of the numbers.

But here's the thing: the success of this step depends entirely on the foundation you've already laid. Like a golfer who's taken the time to adjust their stance, grip and alignment, the effort you put into defining data needs, acquiring the right sources and preparing the data ensures that this step delivers meaningful results. Without that preparation, your analysis, no matter how sophisticated, risks being inaccurate or irrelevant.

The goal of analysis isn't just to find answers; it's to interpret what the data is telling you in a way that supports decisions and drives action. Let's break this step into clear, manageable stages.

Before diving into charts and numbers, clarify what you're trying to uncover. Analysis without direction can lead you down rabbit holes, wasting time on insights that don't align with your objectives.

Start by revisiting the questions and goals you established in Step 1. For example: 'Why are employees leaving the company? Are specific departments or factors driving higher turnover rates?'

Having these questions front and centre keeps you focused and ensures your analysis serves a purpose and the type of analysis you conduct depends on the questions you're trying to answer. Broadly, analysis falls into four main categories:

1 **Descriptive analysis:** Summarizes what happened. Example: 'Turnover increased by 15 per cent in the last 12 months.'

2 **Diagnostic analysis:** Explains why something happened. Example: 'Turnover is higher in departments with low supervisor ratings.'

3 **Predictive analysis:** Forecasts what is likely to happen. Example: 'Employees with low engagement scores are 20 per cent more likely to leave within six months.'

4 **Prescriptive analysis:** Suggests actions to improve outcomes. Example: 'Targeted leadership training could reduce turnover by 10 per cent.'

This book focuses on descriptive and diagnostic analysis. The latter two, predictive and prescriptive, are more advanced and beyond the scope of what we can cover here.

To get a feel for the data, exploring the data helps to identify patterns, relationships and outliers. At this stage, you're looking for insights that answer your analytical questions or reveal unexpected findings.

For instance, in our HR example, you might compare turnover rates across departments, roles or tenure to identify where the problems are most concentrated, allowing you to start interpreting what the data is telling you. This is where analysis becomes meaningful. Data alone doesn't tell the whole story; it's your interpretation that turns numbers into insights that drive action and helps us get answers as to why something is happening and what the implications are.

Be careful not to jump to conclusions or overgeneralize. Always ground your interpretation in the data and acknowledge any limitations (e.g. sample size, missing data).

Step 5: communication and influencing decisions

The final stretch of the data interpretation journey is where insights meet action. Analysing the data and uncovering insights is only part of the process. For your work to create impact, you need to communicate those findings effectively and influence others to act on them. Like a golfer's follow-through, this step ensures your efforts don't stop short but drive meaningful results.

Everything that comes before this can be argued as the domain for developing your technical competence, with the possible exception of the first step. However, many data professionals fall short of influencing their stakeholders. That is the reason why a whole step in this process is dedicated to addressing the last mile so that you can ensure you make your message heard and action is taken.

No matter how strong your analysis is, it won't make a difference if your stakeholders don't understand it, or worse, don't act on it. Communicating insights isn't just about sharing charts, graphs or numbers; it's about creating a bridge between the data and its informed decisions. Your role as a communicator is to ensure the audience sees the story within the data and understands how it applies to them.

When done well, effective communication ensures your stakeholders will quickly grasp the key insights, ideally without confusion. They should care about the findings because they directly connect to their priorities and goals and, when delivered well, the audience will know what action they need to take and who is accountable for that action.

First, understanding your audience is essential. Tailor your communication to their needs, priorities and level of data literacy, ensuring that your message resonates and is easily understood. Simplifying the story is equally important; rather than overwhelming your audience with excessive detail, focus on the core message to make your insights clear and impactful. Presenting your insights as a narrative can be particularly powerful. Structuring your communication around a problem-insight-resolution framework provides a logical flow that highlights the issue, explains the key findings and proposes actionable solutions.

For example, you might start by identifying the problem, such as, 'Employee turnover has increased by 15 per cent over the last year.' Then, you could present the insight: 'Turnover rates are highest in departments with low supervisor ratings and low engagement scores.' Finally, propose a resolution: 'By implementing targeted leadership training and engagement initiatives, we can reduce turnover and save $500,000 annually.'

By framing your communication as a compelling story, you engage your audience, emphasize the significance of the findings and make your recommendations both memorable and actionable. This approach not only conveys your insights but also motivates decision-makers to take meaningful steps based on the data.

Communication and influence are the golfer's follow-through, ensuring that the effort you've put into defining, acquiring and analysing data achieves its full potential. Without clear communication, your insights risk being misunderstood or ignored. Without influencing action, even the most compelling recommendations will remain unrealized potential.

Here's the payoff: when stakeholders understand your insights, trust your recommendations and see the value of acting on them, you create lasting impact. Over time, this positions you as a trusted voice in the organization, someone who not only works with data but makes it matter.

The ultimate test of your work is whether it drives measurable change. Keep an eye on the outcomes of your recommendations: Are key metrics improving? Are stakeholders implementing the changes you suggested? Is the organization moving closer to its goals?

If not, revisit the earlier steps in the process. Perhaps the data wasn't quite right, or the communication didn't resonate as intended. The data interpretation journey is iterative, and learning from feedback is part of the process.

The journey to action

Now that you're familiar with the steps of the data interpretation journey, it's time to connect the dots and understand the bigger picture. Each stage builds on the last, creating a clear path from defining the right questions to influencing decisions. While this process is the one we focus on in this book, it's important to note that there are many ways to work with data. No matter which approach you follow, success always depends on three core principles: 1) setting clear objectives aligned with your goals; 2) spending time on preparing and understanding the data; and 3) communicating insights effectively to drive action.

Where most processes fall short is at the final step: communication. This is often the hardest part of working with data, yet it's the most critical. Without action, insights remain untapped potential, like a golfer who stops swinging just before the follow-through. To stand out, you must go beyond analysis and ensure your work leads to measurable results.

This book will help you develop skills at every stage of the process, but the last step is where the true impact happens. The more disruptive or unexpected your findings, the more resistance you may face. The ability to guide others through that discomfort, to inspire trust and to overcome inertia is what will set you apart.

As we dive deeper into each stage in the coming chapters, keep the entire journey in mind. Each step is a building block, and skipping one can undermine the rest. Success with data is not just about uncovering insights, it's about making sure those insights drive meaningful action.

Now, let's bring the process to life by revisiting our HR example from Chapter 1. We'll walk through each step – defining data needs, acquisition, preparation, analysis and finally communication and influence – to see how the pieces come together to reduce employee turnover and deliver real business value.

Example

Let's revisit the HR analytics scenario introduced in Chapter 1 and plan how to tackle the challenge of reducing employee turnover. As the data analyst for your mid-sized company, you'll be guiding the team through the data interpretation journey to uncover insights and drive actionable change. While we'll dive into the details of each step in later chapters, this example will outline how you might plan for the process as a whole.

The company has observed a concerning increase in employee turnover rates over the past year. Leadership has tasked you and the HR team with identifying the reasons behind this trend and proposing data-driven solutions to improve retention.

Successfully addressing this challenge requires a structured approach. Here's how you plan to navigate the five key steps:

1　**Defining data needs:** You'll start by working with the HR team to clearly define the business goal: reduce employee turnover.

To achieve this, you'll need to determine the key questions to answer, such as:

o Which departments or roles are experiencing the highest turnover?

o Are there patterns related to supervisor performance, training hours or tenure?

o What other factors might signal dissatisfaction or disengagement?

From these questions, you'll identify the metrics to analyse and ensure they align directly with the business goal.

2 **Data acquisition:** You'll identify the data sources needed to answer these questions, such as HR systems, engagement surveys and performance management tools. Part of your plan involves collaborating with other teams to access the data and ensuring compliance with privacy and governance policies. You'll also anticipate challenges, like navigating siloed systems or incomplete datasets, and have a plan for addressing them.

3 **Data preparation:** Once the data is gathered, you'll need to prepare it for analysis. This step involves cleaning the data to address missing values, removing duplicates and ensuring consistency across formats. You'll also plan to integrate data from multiple sources into a single dataset, ready for exploration. By preparing in advance, you'll avoid common pitfalls that can derail analysis later.

4 **Data analysis:** With the prepared dataset, you'll conduct exploratory analysis to uncover trends, patterns and relationships. Your plan includes focusing on actionable insights, such as identifying specific factors contributing to turnover and using these findings to support recommendations. While predictive or prescriptive techniques might come later, you'll start by addressing the most pressing diagnostic questions.

5 **Communication and influencing decisions:** The final step in your plan is to ensure your findings drive action. You'll outline how you'll present insights to leadership, focusing on clarity, relevance and actionability. This involves crafting a narrative that ties data findings to the company's goals, using visuals like charts to highlight key points, and proposing clear, evidence-based recommendations.

This example highlights the importance of approaching data interpretation as a process. By planning for each step, you ensure that your analysis stays aligned with the company's goals, avoids common challenges and delivers actionable results.

In the coming chapters, we'll explore each step in more detail, equipping you with the tools to confidently understand data projects that make an impact. For now, think of this as your roadmap, a structured approach to turn data into decisions.

Exercise

Think about a business problem you're facing in your organization.

- What would your **Step 1: Defining data needs** look like?
- What questions would you need to answer?
- Which metrics would you identify to address those questions?
- Where might you acquire that data?

Take 5–10 minutes to sketch out the starting point for your own data interpretation journey. You don't need all the answers yet; focus on defining the problem and identifying the potential data sources.

Summary points

- **Defining your purpose**
  Start every data project by clarifying what questions you need answered and how the answers will support business goals.

- **Getting the right data**
  Acquiring accurate and relevant data can be challenging, but investing in the right sources upfront saves time and effort later.

- **Preparing your data**
  Clean, integrate and standardize your data before analysis. Good preparation ensures reliable insights and avoids misleading results.

- **Focused analysis**
  Let your initial questions guide your analytical approach. Whether you're looking at descriptive trends or exploring deeper patterns, stay aligned with your objectives.

- **Communicating for action**
  Insights mean little if they're not understood or implemented. Present findings clearly, tailor your message to the audience and be prepared to guide stakeholders toward informed decisions.

Part 2
Defining data needs

03
Asking the right questions

Mapping the path forward

Picture yourself without your mobile phone, standing at a cross-roads with a detailed, printed map in hand. The map brims with information, including roads, landmarks and countless details, yet it's not very helpful without a clear sense of where you want to go. You might ask, 'Which way leads north?' or 'Is this path steeper than the others?' While these questions yield facts, they don't help you decide where you should head or why. It's only by asking the right questions – 'Where am I trying to get to?' and 'What do I hope to achieve once I'm there?' that the map becomes truly valuable. The right questions turn raw information into a guide.

The same principle applies to interpreting data in business. Data alone can show you trends, patterns and anomalies, but it won't reveal your best course of action unless you ask the right questions. Without a straightforward, purposeful question aligned with your strategic goals, even the richest datasets remain silent on what you should actually do.

In this chapter, we build on your previous work in defining your data needs. We'll focus on how to craft compelling, actionable questions. These questions serve as a guiding vision, ensuring that as your organization matures in using data, the insights you uncover are not just interesting but also aligned with where you want the business to go.

The power of a well-formulated question

A well-crafted question acts like a compass for your data journey. It points you toward what you need to find out and why it matters, ensuring you don't just wander through data but move forward with purpose. Without strong, goal-oriented questions, even the richest datasets remain an untapped resource, i.e. lots of numbers but no clear direction.

When you set a focused question at the outset, you make the data more relatable and accessible. Framing your inquiry as a clear question removes unnecessary complexity and avoids technical jargon, instead presenting a business-friendly challenge that everyone can understand. A well-defined question also outlines the exact kind of data you need. Rather than collecting everything in the hope that something useful will emerge, you can identify the specific metrics or data sources that are relevant from the start.

Additionally, focused questions guide analysis by aligning your approach with the problem at hand. For instance, asking how sales changed month-over-month leads naturally to time-series analysis, whereas exploring the drivers of customer churn directs you to examine behaviours and attributes that predict departures. These questions also sharpen interpretation by helping you filter out irrelevant data, clarifying which insights are critical and ensuring your conclusions remain aligned with the organization's objectives.

Effective questions do not exist in isolation. They must connect to your organization's strategy and drive actionable steps. Think of it as a journey: starting with strategy and ending with action, the question serves as the bridge between these points. This ensures that the data you collect and interpret is not just interesting but is also capable of informing decisions that create meaningful impact.

Too often, teams focus on the data itself, collecting as much as possible, hoping insights will emerge. This 'analysis paralysis' wastes effort. With a well-framed question, you direct your data work towards a clear goal, making your findings more impactful.

Figure 3.1   Strategic alignment

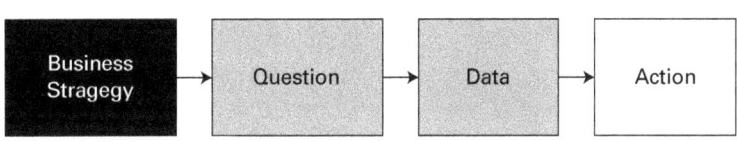

Ultimately, success with data is as much about people as it is about numbers. Formulating questions that everyone understands and cares about encourages collaboration across departments. It can be uncomfortable; stakeholders must engage, debate priorities and refine their inquiries. However, it's far more effective than working in isolation and hoping valuable insights magically appear.

By starting with a strategic question and ending with data-informed action, you adhere to a streamlined process. It sounds straightforward but it takes practice and a commitment to focus on what truly needs to be answered.

Crafting an effective question

An effective question creates a clear path from business strategy to actionable insights. By defining what you need to know and how it aligns with your goals, you can ensure that any insights gained lead to meaningful change. To achieve this, it is essential to consider several key elements when formulating a question.

Your question should align closely with the organization's core business objectives. For instance, if your company is focused on improving customer loyalty, the question should directly address factors influencing retention. Specificity and clarity are also critical; vague questions lead to vague answers. Clearly defining the scope – such as timeframes, regions, products or customer segments – ensures targeted data collection and focused analysis. For example, asking, 'What factors contributed to the 8 per cent decline in online sales of our premium product line in North

America during Q3 compared to Q2?' provides the detail necessary for actionable insights.

Actionability is another essential component. A strong question doesn't just uncover what happened but guides the next steps. For example, a question like, 'What improvements can we make to reduce average support resolution time by 20 per cent in the next six months?' directs efforts toward strategic changes rather than passive observation. Measurability is equally important; questions should include quantifiable elements such as percentages, timeframes or other metrics to track progress. Asking, 'How can we increase our social media engagement rate by 15 per cent over the next quarter among users aged 18–24?' provides a clear goal and criteria for success.

To avoid assumptions and bias, frame your questions openly. Instead of asking, 'Why is our outdated website causing a drop in sales?', which presumes a cause, ask, 'What factors are contributing to the 10 per cent decrease in online sales over the past two months?' This neutral approach ensures that the analysis is grounded in data rather than preconceived notions. Additionally, it is important to maintain a singular focus, addressing one issue at a time. While sub-questions are acceptable, handling them individually ensures precision and usability. For example, asking, 'What are the most common reasons for product returns in our electronics category over the past year?' focuses on one specific area for analysis.

Finally, ensure your question is relevant to stakeholders who will act on the insights. A question that resonates with key decision-makers increases the likelihood of your results driving action. For example, 'Which marketing channels have generated the highest ROI for our new product launch in Europe, and how can we allocate budget to maximize returns in Q4?' directly helps the marketing team prioritize efforts effectively.

These elements work together to create questions that produce meaningful insights and lead to informed decisions and tangible improvements. Broad or misaligned inquiries can waste time and resources, while focused, well-crafted questions set the foundation for impactful analysis.

Broad, vague or misaligned questions can hinder meaningful analysis, but refining them ensures clarity and relevance. For example, a broad question like 'Why are our profits decreasing?' lacks context and direction. By narrowing the focus to something like 'Which product categories have seen the largest profit declines over the past quarter?' you provide analysts with a clear path forward. Similarly, questions that don't align with strategic goals can divert attention. If the company's priority is enhancing customer satisfaction, a question such as 'How can we reduce production costs?' may be less relevant than 'What cost reductions can we implement without impacting customer experience?'

Ambiguity also weakens the value of questions. A vague inquiry like 'How can we become the best in the industry?' lacks defined targets. A stronger approach would be 'What steps can we take to increase customer retention by 15 per cent within a year compared to industry benchmarks?' Effective questions are specific, measurable and actionable, connecting insights to strategic actions.

Refining questions involves adding clarity, context and measurable goals. For example, changing 'Why are employees leaving?' to 'What factors have caused a 15 per cent increase in turnover among our software development team over the past year, and how can we reduce turnover by 10 per cent in six months?' ties the analysis to actionable outcomes. Strong questions not only guide data analysis but also ensure efforts lead to impactful and strategic results.

Measuring success and action

Asking the right questions sets the stage for meaningful analysis, but questions alone are not enough. To measure the success of our efforts and determine whether actions are being taken based on the data, we need to translate those questions into key performance indicators (KPIs).

A KPI is more than just a metric; it's a measurable target that links your questions and goals to actionable outcomes. While a metric might answer 'What is happening?', a KPI provides a benchmark for success and progress toward a specific goal.

For example:

- **Question:** What is driving employee turnover in the Sales department?
- **Goal:** Reduce turnover by 15 per cent in the next year.
- **KPI:** Quarterly turnover rate in the Sales department.

KPIs act as a proxy for action in many situations. If a KPI improves, it often reflects that the recommended actions from your analysis are being implemented effectively. In cases where direct measurement of action is difficult, KPIs provide an indirect way to monitor progress and ensure your work is driving results.

While KPIs are pivotal for measuring outcomes, they are not always required, especially in exploratory analysis. Defining KPIs upfront may limit creativity and discovery when exploring new datasets or looking for unexpected patterns. In such cases, focus on understanding the data's structure and generating hypotheses rather than setting rigid benchmarks.

However, when analysis shifts towards action, making decisions or solving problems, KPIs become essential. They clarify whether your insights are driving the intended changes and help keep stakeholders aligned with organizational goals.

Effective KPIs share key characteristics that ensure they remain impactful and aligned with organizational goals. First, KPIs must be actionable, prompting decisions when trends or changes occur. For instance, a rising turnover rate in the Sales department should trigger interventions like enhanced training or revised management practices. They must also be measurable, such as a specific goal like 'Increase engagement scores by 10 per cent'. Relevance is equally important; KPIs should directly connect to the objectives they aim to measure. For example, tracking coffee consumption in the breakroom has no bearing on reducing employee turnover.

Timeliness is another critical feature; data must be updated frequently enough to support decision-making in real time. Finally, KPIs should be clear and easily understood by all stakeholders without requiring extensive explanation.

KPIs can be categorized into two types: leading indicators, which are forward-looking and help predict potential outcomes, and lagging indicators, which reflect past performance. For example, engagement survey results may serve as a leading indicator, signalling future turnover trends, while an annual turnover rate acts as a lagging indicator, summarizing past performance. Striking a balance between leading and lagging indicators enables proactive measures while validating the effectiveness of past actions.

By keeping your analysis focused on the most relevant questions and goals, KPIs help ensure actionable insights. For instance, if a KPI shows rising turnover, it might prompt deeper analysis into related metrics like engagement scores or supervisor ratings. Consistently aligning KPIs with your initial questions ensures that your analysis remains goal-oriented and continues to drive meaningful and actionable insights.

Frameworks for crafting questions

Like several other elements in working with people and data, crafting an effective question is both art and science. While understanding the key characteristics of good questions is essential, leveraging a structured framework can greatly enhance your ability to formulate questions that drive meaningful insights and actions. Two widely recognized frameworks are the SMART criteria and the 5 Whys technique.

The SMART criteria

Originally popular in project management and goal setting, the SMART framework is a powerful approach for refining your business questions. The framework was first introduced in 1981 by George T Doran in his paper 'There's a S.M.A.R.T. way to write management's goals and objectives', published in *Management Review*. SMART stands for:

- **Specific:** Clearly define what you want to address. Rather than asking, 'How do we improve sales?', pinpoint the product, audience and region you're concerned with.

- **Measurable:** Set clear metrics to know when you've achieved your goal. A target percentage or a timeline provides a benchmark for success.

- **Attainable:** Ensure the goal is realistic, given your resources and data availability. Don't aim for a metric that far exceeds historical precedent without good reason.

- **Relevant:** Align the question with your overarching strategy. If your priority is customer satisfaction, a question about cutting costs diverts attention from the main objective.

- **Time-bound:** Give yourself a deadline. A defined timeframe keeps everyone focused and prevents indefinite analysis.

Using the SMART framework can turn a broad, vague inquiry into a well-defined question that directs what data to gather and how to measure progress. For example, if you start with 'How can we improve online sales?', applying SMART might lead you to ask, 'What marketing strategies can we implement to increase online sales of our eco-friendly product line among urban millennials by 15 per cent within the next quarter?'

This structured approach encourages clarity from the start. It also helps stakeholders agree on the question's scope and feasibility before you invest in data collection and analysis. While SMART is widely known and easy to adopt, it's not the only technique available. Another powerful tool for sharpening questions and uncovering underlying issues is the 5 Whys technique.

Figure 3.2 The SMART framework

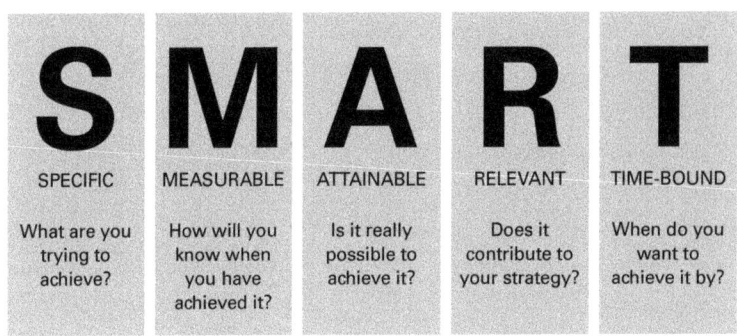

S	M	A	R	T
SPECIFIC	MEASURABLE	ATTAINABLE	RELEVANT	TIME-BOUND
What are you trying to achieve?	How will you know when you have achieved it?	Is it really possible to achieve it?	Does it contribute to your strategy?	When do you want to achieve it by?

The 5 Whys technique

Sometimes, your initial question only scratches the surface of a problem. The 5 Whys technique offers a simple method to peel back layers until you reach the core issue. By asking 'Why?' repeatedly, often around five times, you move beyond immediate symptoms and uncover the root cause. It was originally developed by Sakichi Toyoda and was famously implemented in the Toyota Production System by Taichi Ohno.

Here's how it works in practice:

1 **First why (surface level):** Start with the obvious question, such as 'Why did sales drop?' You'll likely get an immediate reason: maybe a marketing campaign underperformed.

2 **Second why (dig deeper):** Don't stop. Ask 'Why didn't the campaign perform well?' The response could be that the team didn't target the right audience.

3 **Third why (investigate factors):** Continue with 'Why didn't we target the right audience?' Perhaps because there wasn't sufficient data to inform decisions.

4 **Fourth why (peel away layers):** Now ask 'Why didn't we have the right data?' Maybe data collection processes were never set up, or key metrics weren't tracked.

5 **Fifth why (core cause):** Finally, 'Why weren't those processes established?' At this point, you might discover a fundamental gap in data strategy or accountability that must be addressed.

Figure 3.3   The 5 Whys technique

Each 'Why?' takes you closer to the actual root of the problem. Often, you won't need all five steps, but the principle remains: don't settle for the first answer. The 5 Whys technique helps ensure your eventual question targets a deeper, more meaningful issue. Once you identify the root cause, you can apply the SMART framework to refine and focus your question, turning a general inquiry into a precise, measurable and achievable one.

Practical steps to formulate questions

We've covered why good questions matter, explored what makes them effective and introduced frameworks like SMART and the 5 Whys. Now, let's translate theory into action. The following steps guide you from initial strategic goals to well-formed, actionable questions that everyone can rally around.

1. Start with business objectives

Every question should stem from the organization's core priorities. If your top goal is improving customer satisfaction, avoid drifting into unrelated territory. Ask yourself: What does the business really need to achieve? Is it boosting retention, increasing revenue in a specific product line or enhancing operational efficiency? Applying the SMART criteria here ensures that each question is aligned, measurable and time-bound, directly reinforcing strategic aims.

2. Engage stakeholders

Effective questions rarely emerge in isolation. Collaborate with team members from different departments. Their insights can reveal overlooked factors or confirm that the question resonates across the organization. Techniques like brainstorming sessions or using the 5 Whys with a diverse group can pinpoint underlying issues. When multiple voices shape the question, you're more likely to address the real problem and find actionable solutions.

3. Prioritize your questions

Not all questions carry the same weight. Some may lead to quick wins and tangible improvements in a short timeframe, while others are longer term and more complex. Consider both impact and feasibility. If data availability or resources are limited, refine the question using SMART to ensure it's realistic. Balancing quick wins with strategic challenges can build momentum and sustained support for your data initiatives.

4. Iterate and refine

Formulating questions isn't a one-and-done task. As you gain insights from data, new questions emerge or old ones need adjustment. Keep revisiting and refining your inquiries. Maybe the initial target was too ambitious, or new market conditions change what's relevant. Using both SMART and the 5 Whys techniques over time helps maintain clarity and keeps your questions focused on evolving business goals.

Example

Let's build on the HR analytics scenario introduced previously. As a data analyst tasked with reducing employee turnover, your first step is to refine your understanding of the problem by asking targeted, strategic questions. This chapter focuses on the planning and structure of those questions, ensuring they align with business goals and drive meaningful analysis.

The strategic goal is to reduce turnover in the software development team by 10 per cent within six months. Leadership has tasked you with identifying why employees are leaving and what actionable steps can be taken to improve retention. The initial, broad question, 'Why are employees leaving?' is a good starting point but lacks the specificity needed for focused analysis. Your task is to refine this question to guide your data efforts.

To ensure your efforts align with the organization's strategy and lead to actionable insights, you begin refining the broad question using the techniques covered in this chapter.

Step 1: Apply the 5 Whys technique

You start by digging deeper into the root cause of the problem:

1 **Why are employees leaving?**
   Because they're dissatisfied.

2 **Why are they dissatisfied?**
   Because they feel there's a lack of career growth.

3 **Why is there a lack of career growth?**
   Because training and promotion opportunities are limited.

4 **Why are training and promotion opportunities limited?**
   Because the company hasn't invested enough in structured
   career development programmes.

This iterative process reveals that the core issue isn't just
dissatisfaction; it's the perception that career advancement
opportunities are lacking.

Step 2: Use the SMART framework

Now, you refine the question further using the SMART criteria:

- **Specific:** Focus on the software development team and
  career growth opportunities.

- **Measurable:** Set a clear target: reduce turnover by 10 per
  cent within six months.

- **Achievable:** Ensure the target is realistic based on past
  trends and available resources.

- **Relevant:** Align the question with the company's strategic goal
  of retaining top talent.

- **Time-bound:** Provide a defined timeline of six months.

Refined question: 'What career development initiatives can we
implement for the software development team to reduce turnover
by 10 per cent within the next six months?'

With a clear question in place, you can now plan what data to
collect. The refined question guides you to focus on the following
key data points:

- **Employee engagement survey results:** Insights into
  perceptions of career growth and satisfaction.

- **Training and promotion records:** Frequency and availability of
  training programmes and promotions over the past year.

- **Exit interview data:** Reasons cited by departing employees,
  particularly related to career advancement.

- **Turnover metrics:** Current turnover rates in the software
  development team for benchmarking progress.

The refined question also points to specific actions you can take once the data is analysed. For example:

- **Introduce tailored training programmes:** Based on gaps identified in the data.

- **Implement structured promotion pathways:** Ensure employees have visibility into growth opportunities.

- **Launch mentorship initiatives:** Pair junior employees with senior staff to foster career development and engagement.

Tying the question to actionable outcomes ensures that your analysis will directly contribute to achieving the organization's strategic goal.

This example highlights the importance of formulating practical questions at the outset of a data project. A vague question like 'Why are employees leaving?' leads to scattered efforts and unfocused analysis. However, techniques like the 5 Whys and the SMART framework transform a broad inquiry into a specific, actionable question that sets the foundation for impactful data analysis.

In the following chapters, we'll dive deeper into how to execute each stage of the data interpretation process, using this refined question as a guide. For now, remember: the quality of your insights depends on the quality of your questions. Investing time upfront to craft well-structured questions will pay dividends throughout the rest of the process.

Exercise

1   Take a vague business question relevant to your organization, something like 'How can we increase revenue?' or 'Why are customers unhappy?'

2   Apply the **5 Whys** to uncover deeper root causes.

3 Use the **SMART framework** to transform the initial vague question into a specific, measurable, achievable, relevant and time-bound inquiry.

4 Write down the final refined question and identify at least two data points you would need to answer it.

Summary points

- **Start with strategy**
  Ensure every question aligns with overarching business goals, keeping data efforts on track.

- **Be specific and measurable**
  Vague questions lead to vague answers. Introduce metrics, timeframes and well-defined scopes.

- **Use frameworks**
  The SMART criteria and 5 Whys techniques help refine questions, uncover root causes and ensure questions are both actionable and realistic.

- **Collaborate and iterate**
  Involve stakeholders to gain multiple perspectives and be ready to revisit and refine questions as new insights emerge.

- **End with action**
  The ultimate purpose of well-crafted questions is to guide meaningful decisions and improvements, turning data into genuine business value.

04
Turning questions into requirements

Assembling your ingredients

Imagine you're a chef preparing a signature dish for a high-profile event. You've carefully chosen your recipe – this represents the question you formed in the previous chapter. The recipe lists ingredients and instructions, but before you can start cooking, you need to gather the right ingredients from reliable sources. Some ingredients are common pantry staples, while others might require a trip to a speciality market. You may even need to place a special order if the ingredient is rare or seasonal.

In much the same way, once you have your well-defined question, the next step is to find and assemble the data that will help you answer it. Just as a chef checks the freshness and quality of each ingredient, you'll need to confirm data availability, ensure its accuracy and consider the context (like timeframes or customer segments) to make it meaningful.

This chapter guides you through the data acquisition process. You'll learn how to break down your question into precise data requirements, locate the best sources, navigate access permissions, add context for clearer insights and validate your data so you can trust the final result. By following a structured approach – like the BRICE framework – you'll set yourself up to 'cook' a truly impactful analysis, turning raw data into valuable, actionable insights.

Figure 4.1   Identifying data sources from questions

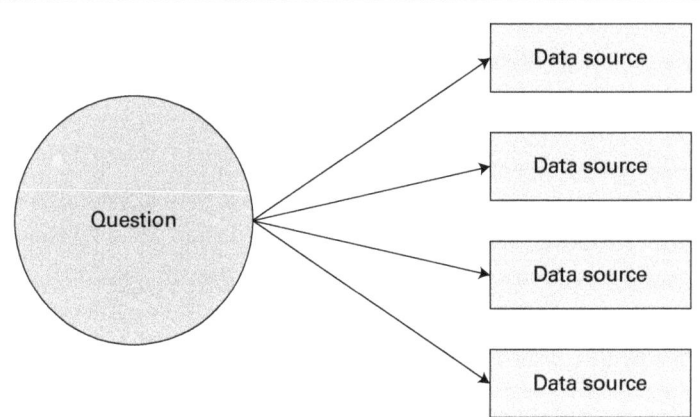

Questions guide data acquisition

In Chapter 3, you refined your questions until they were tightly aligned with business objectives, clear, specific and ready to guide meaningful action. Now comes the practical part: finding and preparing the right data to answer those questions.

Without a plan, data acquisition can become an overwhelming scavenger hunt. You might end up collecting data that's irrelevant or too large in scope, leading to 'analysis paralysis' where you're drowning in numbers but can't find insights that matter. A structured approach ensures that every piece of data you gather directly supports your question, helping you avoid wasted effort and focus on what's truly impactful.

By using your carefully crafted question as a compass, you'll know exactly what kind of data you need, where it might reside and how to contextualize it so that the final analysis yields actionable recommendations. The BRICE framework offers a systematic, step-by-step method to break down your question, refine metrics, identify sources, contextualize needs and validate what you've collected. Rather than diving blindly into databases and spreadsheets, you'll follow a clear roadmap that leads to meaningful, reliable and timely insights.

The BRICE framework

Having a clear, well-defined question is just the beginning. Now you need a structured method to transform that question into a precise set of data requirements. This is where the BRICE framework comes in. BRICE stands for:

B: Break down the question

R: Refine the elements

I: Identify data sources

C: Contextualize data needs

E: Extract and validate data

By following these five steps in order, you ensure that your data acquisition remains aligned with the original business question. Instead of haphazardly collecting whatever data you can find, BRICE guides you to systematically clarify what you need, determine where it resides, factor in timing and segmentation, and verify its quality. The result is a more efficient path to meaningful, actionable insights.

Step 1: Break down the question

Before you can gather data, you must understand exactly what you're looking for. Even a well-formed question often contains multiple underlying components that need to be explored. The first step in the BRICE framework, 'Break down the question', helps you identify these components and anticipate the data required for meaningful analysis.

For example, if your question is, 'What factors are influencing the decline in customer retention rates over the past year?' you

Figure 4.2   The BRICE process

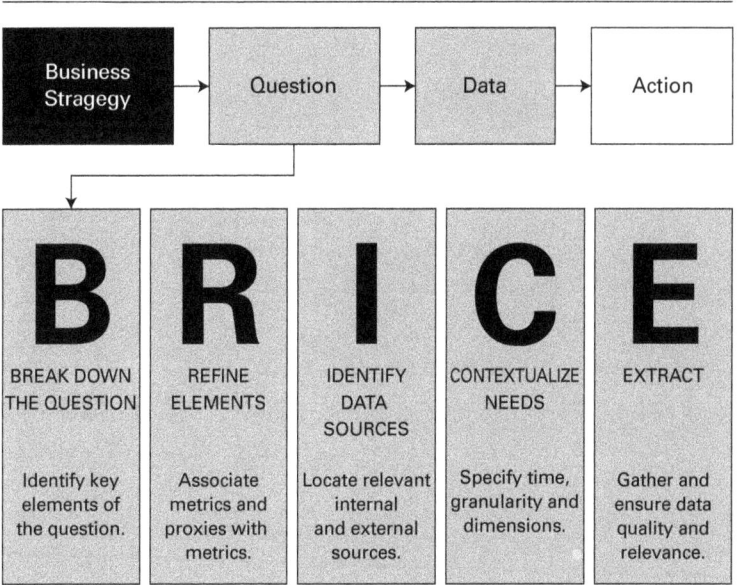

should consider a range of possible influences. These might include customer behaviour, such as purchase frequency, repeat purchases and average order value; service issues, like support response times, resolution rates and feedback scores; and product quality and satisfaction, which could involve return rates, defect rates and survey results. By breaking the question into these distinct elements, you gain a clearer picture of the data you need, ensuring that key details are not overlooked and that unnecessary information is avoided.

When direct measures for certain components are unavailable, it is important to think creatively about proxies. For instance, if 'service quality' is not directly measured, you might combine related metrics such as support response times and survey feedback to construct a meaningful stand-in. This approach ensures that your data collection remains both comprehensive and targeted, setting the stage for effective analysis.

Step 2: Refine the elements

After breaking down the question into components, the next step is to refine these elements into measurable metrics. This process involves translating each factor into specific, actionable data points. For example, if one component is 'customer behaviour', relevant metrics could include purchase frequency, which tracks how often each customer buys within a given timeframe; average order value, reflecting the typical spend per transaction; and repeat purchase rate, showing the percentage of customers who return.

Refining elements into clear metrics helps you ensure every aspect of the question is quantifiable and directly tied to your organization's strategic goals. This approach not only facilitates meaningful analysis but also focuses efforts on insights that are both relevant and actionable. Additionally, identifying key performance indicators (KPIs) that align with strategic objectives can provide a valuable compass for guiding your analysis. As discussed in Chapter 3, KPIs measure progress towards key goals and help ensure that your efforts are directed at what matters most.

Step 3: Identify data sources

Once you've identified the key metrics, the next step is determining where to find them. Metrics may reside in various systems or even outside your organization, making the identification of data sources a crucial part of the process. Internal systems such as CRM platforms or sales databases can provide insights into customer behaviour, helpdesk platforms are useful for support metrics and product management databases often contain data on defect or return rates. External sources, like third-party market research, industry benchmarks or social listening tools, can supplement internal data, especially when gaps exist.

Mapping each metric to a specific source streamlines data collection, reducing the time spent searching and allowing you to focus on confirming availability and securing access. Understanding your data landscape early ensures you can manage expectations and account for any permissions, technical integrations or additional data collection efforts required. This preparation sets a solid foundation for efficient and effective analysis.

Step 4: Contextualize data needs

Once you've identified the metrics and their sources, the next step is to establish the context in which these metrics will be analysed. Contextualizing data involves defining the time period, level of detail, segmentation and attributes that will frame your analysis. Without this context, even accurate metrics can be misinterpreted, leading to misguided conclusions.

Start by specifying the time period relevant to your question. For example, if you're analysing customer retention over the past year, use a 12-month window and consider monthly snapshots to uncover seasonal trends. Next, identify the attributes and segments that matter most. Examining meaningful subsets, such as loyal customers versus new ones or specific product categories, allows you to pinpoint which groups drive observed trends. Finally, determine the appropriate level of granularity. While daily data might be overly detailed and obscure broader patterns, monthly summaries often provide clearer strategic insights. Choose the level of detail that aligns with the scope of your analysis.

By defining timeframes, attributes, segments and granularity, you transform raw data into meaningful, actionable insights. This ensures that every data point contributes to a coherent understanding of the issue at hand, preventing wasted effort on irrelevant details or overlooked patterns.

Step 5: Extract and validate data

With your sources identified and context defined, the next step is to extract and validate your data. Extraction involves retrieving data from the specified systems, whether through SQL queries, API calls, CSV exports or data integration tools. Validation ensures that the data you've gathered is accurate, complete and ready for analysis.

Begin by checking for completeness to confirm that all necessary fields and time periods are represented. Missing data in critical metrics, such as satisfaction scores, can skew your results. Consistency is also key: formats must match across sources, with dates, currency values and units standardized for meaningful comparisons. Ensure the data's relevance by verifying that it aligns with the scope, timeframe and segments of your question, and remove any extraneous information that doesn't contribute to your analysis. Finally, conduct basic accuracy checks by spot-checking values against known benchmarks or internal reports. If discrepancies arise, investigate and resolve them before proceeding.

Validation acts as a crucial quality assurance step, preventing the 'garbage in, garbage out' scenarios that can undermine your analysis. By ensuring the data is reliable and well prepared, you set the foundation for insights that are both accurate and actionable.

The role of relationships and permissions

While the technical aspects of data acquisition are certainly necessary, the human element is equally important. Data often resides in multiple departments, each with its own policies, priorities and permissions. Building strong relationships with data owners and custodians can significantly streamline access and simplify the process of obtaining essential information.

Start by communicating early with data owners. As soon as you know what you need, reach out and explain the business value of your request, linking it to strategic goals to encourage their support. Be mindful of governance policies and demonstrate respect for the responsibilities of data custodians, assuring them that you will handle the information responsibly. Flexibility is also important; if direct access isn't immediately available, consider phased requests or accept aggregated views while negotiating for more comprehensive data. Additionally, document all approvals, data sources and constraints. Keeping a detailed record not only aids future data requests but also ensures transparency and accountability.

By treating data owners as collaborators rather than gatekeepers, you foster trust and create an environment where data flows more freely. This approach not only expedites your current project but also lays the groundwork for smoother data acquisition in the future.

Documenting data requirements

Proper documentation is necessary for maintaining clarity and ensuring that all stakeholders are aligned throughout the data acquisition process. A well-structured data requirements list serves as a blueprint, enabling effective communication with data owners, custodians and technical teams. By clearly defining what data is needed, where to find it and how it will be used, organizations can achieve greater efficiency, accountability and consistency in their data processes.

Clarity is achieved by explicitly outlining the required metrics, sources and contextual details, so all stakeholders share a unified understanding of the data needs. This structured approach creates a roadmap that streamlines data acquisition, reducing ambiguity and making it easier to locate and extract relevant data. Documenting ownership and access permissions enhances accountability, ensuring data custodians are identified and future data requests can be managed seamlessly. Finally, consistent documentation minimizes errors and redundancies, fostering a uniform approach to interpreting and using data across teams.

While often boring, documenting requirements will save you heartache down the road and you don't have to go bananas with it, something as basic as Table 4.1 is so much better than nothing at

Table 4.1 A sample data requirements list

Component	Metric	Primary source	Alternative source	Time period	Granularity	Segmentation
Customer behaviour	Purchase frequency	CRM systems, sales databases	POS or ERP systems	Last 12 months	Monthly	Customer demographics (age, location), product lines
	Average order value (AOV)	CRM systems, e-commerce platforms	ERP or financial systems	Last 12 months	Monthly	Sales channel (online, in-store)
	Repeat purchase rate	CRM systems	Loyalty programme databases	Last 12 months	Quarterly	Customer type (new, returning)
Service issues	Support response times	Helpdesk systems	CRM systems	Last 12 months	Monthly	Customer demographics
	Resolution rates	Customer support platforms	CRM systems	Last 12 months	Monthly	Customer segments

Product quality and satisfaction	Customer support feedback	Feedback and survey tools	Social media reviews	Last 12 months	Monthly	Customer segments
	Defect rate	Quality control systems	ERP systems	Last 12 months	Monthly	Product categories
	Product return rate	Product management databases	ERP returns modules	Last 12 months	Monthly	Product categories
	Customer satisfaction scores	Survey platforms, NPS systems	Customer success team records	Last 12 months	Monthly	Customer segments
	Social media sentiment analysis (proxy)	Social listening tools	AI-powered sentiment analysis	Last 12 months	Monthly	Customer segments

all and it will not take you long. This way, it is easier to share and get others on board.

Example

Let's revisit the HR analytics scenario from Chapter 3. Your question is: 'What career development initiatives can we implement for the software development team to reduce turnover by 10 per cent within the next six months?'

In this chapter, you'll focus on planning to gather the data needed to answer this question. Think of this as creating a shopping list before heading to the store; you're deciding what's needed, where to find it and how to ensure it's fresh and reliable.

B: Break down the question

Start by breaking your question into smaller pieces. Ask yourself, what factors might influence whether a developer stays or leaves? Focus on these key areas:

- **Career growth opportunities:** Are developers getting enough training or promotions?
- **Engagement and satisfaction:** Are they happy with their work environment and opportunities?
- **Work-life balance:** Are workloads reasonable and do they have flexibility in their schedules?

By identifying these areas, you're setting the foundation for the type of data you'll need.

R: Refine the elements

Now, refine these broad areas into specific things you can measure. For example:

- **Career growth:** Track how many developers have been promoted or completed training programmes.

- **Engagement:** Use survey scores or feedback to measure how satisfied employees feel.
- **Work-life balance:** Look at average overtime hours or participation in flexible work policies.

These refined elements ensure that the data you're collecting ties directly back to your question.

I: Identify data sources

Next, identify where to find the information you need.

- **Career growth:** Look in HR systems or training logs.
- **Engagement:** Use employee surveys or exit interviews.
- **Work-life balance**: Access time-tracking tools or project management platforms.

If some data isn't readily available, plan to speak with HR or team leads to find it. Your goal here is to map each metric to a specific data source.

C: Contextualize data needs

Now, add details to define what you're focusing on.

- **Timeframe:** Look at data from the past year to identify recent trends.
- **Segmentation:** Narrow your focus to the software development team specifically.
- **Level of detail:** Use monthly summaries instead of daily data for a clearer picture.

Adding this context helps you avoid wasting time on irrelevant details and ensures you're working with the most meaningful data.

E: Extract and validate data

Finally, plan how to pull and validate the data:

- **Extract:** Pull reports from HR systems, survey tools or time-tracking software.

- **Validate:** Spot-check your data to ensure it's accurate and complete. For example, double-check that it covers the software development team and the defined timeframe.

By validating your data upfront, you ensure that your analysis starts with clean and reliable information.

Using the BRICE framework, you now have a clear plan for gathering the data you need. You've broken the question into manageable parts, identified the metrics you're looking for, mapped them to specific sources and added meaningful context to guide your efforts.

This structured approach keeps you focused on answering your original question and avoids the overwhelm of diving into data without a plan.

In the next chapter, you'll learn how to clean and organize this data so it's ready for analysis. For now, focus on creating clarity in your data-gathering process – it's the foundation of every successful data-driven project.

Exercise

1 **Choose a question:** Select a question from your organization (or use a hypothetical one) that was refined in Chapter 3. For example, 'How can we increase customer retention by 15 per cent in the next year among first-time buyers?'

2 **Apply BRICE:**

   o **Break down:** Identify components affecting retention (e.g. onboarding experience, product satisfaction).

   o **Refine elements:** Turn each component into measurable metrics (e.g. onboarding completion rate, product review scores).

   o **Identify sources:** List where to find each metric (e.g. onboarding metrics in LMS, reviews in survey tools).

o **Contextualize:** Choose timeframes, segments (e.g. first-time buyers) and granularity (monthly or quarterly data).

o **Extract and validate:** Plan how you'll pull and verify the data.

3 **Document:** Record your findings, noting any gaps or required proxies.

By completing this exercise, you'll gain hands-on experience applying BRICE to your own questions, preparing you for real-world data acquisition challenges.

Summary points

- **BRICE = clarity and structure**
  The BRICE framework ensures that data acquisition steps are systematic, keeping your efforts aligned with strategic questions.

- **Start from a refined question**
  Begin with a well-defined question that you know is relevant, measurable and actionable, just as you crafted in Chapter 3.

- **Step-by-step approach**
  Breaking down, refining, identifying sources, contextualizing and validating data prevents overwhelm, guards against irrelevance and maintains data quality.

- **Human factors matter**
  Building positive relationships with data owners and communicating your needs clearly can streamline access and foster trust.

- **Ready for analysis**
  Once you've followed BRICE, you'll have a reliable set of data ready for meaningful interpretation, setting the stage for converting data into decisions.

Part 3
Sourcing and governing data

05

Understanding
data sources

Navigating the data landscape

Imagine once again that you are back on that ship from the start of Chapter 1. This time, you have a compass, a map and a clearer understanding of your destination. Just as a traveller studies a map before starting a new journey, you need a clear grasp of the data sources and types that shape your analytical journey. Without this understanding, you risk getting lost in a maze of formats, sources and constraints that can hinder meaningful insights.

In this chapter, we'll start by exploring the sources of data, distinguishing between internal sources aligned with your organization's operations and external sources that offer valuable outside perspectives. From there, we'll examine the various forms data can take, like structured, unstructured and semi-structured, highlighting how each format influences the tools and techniques you'll use.

We'll also look at the differences between quantitative and qualitative data. Numbers and metrics can reveal trends and measure performance, but understanding the human experiences, opinions and motivations behind those numbers is equally essential. By the time you finish this chapter, you'll have a solid foundation for recognizing the nature of your data and selecting appropriate methods to handle it responsibly and effectively.

This fundamental understanding sets the stage for managing data ethically and complying with regulations, topics we'll cover in the next chapter. As you move forward, remember that the insights you'll eventually derive depend on building from a firm understanding of where your data comes from and what it represents.

Types of data sources

Understanding the origins of your data is fundamental to effective data analysis and decision-making. Data sources can be broadly categorized into **internal** and **external** sources. Each category possesses unique characteristics, advantages and challenges that influence how data is utilized within an organization.

Internal data sources

Internal data sources encompass all data generated and collected within the boundaries of an organization. This data originates from the organization's own operations, processes and interactions, making it highly relevant to the company's specific objectives and activities.

Internal data is intrinsically aligned with the organization's strategic goals and operational processes, providing insights directly tied to the company's performance, employee activities, customer interactions and financial transactions. Organizations have substantial control over internal data, enabling them to enforce stringent data governance policies. This control ensures that data quality standards are maintained and that sensitive information is adequately protected against unauthorized access.

Moreover, because internal data is generated through standardized processes and systems, it tends to exhibit higher consistency. This uniformity facilitates easier integration and analysis across different departments and functions within the organization. Internal data offers highly pertinent insights tailored to the organization's specific needs, enabling more accurate and actionable analyses. Typically stored within the organization's infrastructure, internal data is more readily accessible to authorized personnel, reducing the barriers to data retrieval and usage.

However, while internal data provides deep insights into organizational processes, it may lack external context. This limitation can hinder comprehensive analyses that require an understanding of broader market trends or external factors influencing the business. Additionally, internal data often resides in disparate systems and formats, making integration across different data silos a complex and resource-intensive task. Achieving seamless data interoperability may require significant investment in data integration technologies and processes.

External data sources

External data sources refer to data obtained from outside the organization. This data is generated by external entities such as customers, partners, government agencies and the general public. External data complements internal data by providing broader context and benchmarking opportunities.

External data enriches internal datasets by offering insights into market conditions, competitor performance and industry benchmarks. This broader perspective enables organizations to position themselves more effectively within their respective markets. Additionally, external data encompasses a wide range of formats and types, including social media interactions, public records, economic indicators and more. This diversity allows for multifaceted analyses that consider various external influences on the organization.

Furthermore, external data sources are often more dynamic, reflecting real-time changes in the market, consumer behaviour and regulatory environments. This evolving nature requires organizations to continuously monitor and update their external data inputs to maintain relevance. Incorporating external data provides a more comprehensive understanding of the factors affecting the organization, enabling more strategic and informed decision-making.

External data allows organizations to compare their performance against industry standards and competitors, identifying areas of strength and opportunities for improvement. By integrating external trends and indicators, organizations can improve the accuracy of their predictive models, anticipating market shifts and consumer behaviour more effectively.

However, not all external data may directly apply to the organization's context. Careful evaluation is necessary to ensure that the external data aligns with the business questions and objectives at hand. The quality of external data can vary significantly depending on the source. Organizations must assess the external data's credibility, accuracy and timeliness to avoid incorporating flawed or misleading information into their analyses. Accessing high-quality external data often involves costs, whether through subscriptions, licensing fees or data acquisition services. Additionally, some external data sources may have restricted access or usage rights, limiting their availability for organizational use.

Types of data

Data comes in many shapes and sizes, each requiring different approaches for effective analysis and utilization. At a high level, data can be categorized as structured, unstructured or semi-structured. Understanding these distinctions is crucial, as it dictates how you interact with the data, the tools you use and the insights you can derive.

Imagine your data library. Structured data is like a well-organized bookshelf where each book is correctly labelled and categorized by genre, author and year of publication. Finding a specific book is straightforward because everything follows a predictable order. In contrast, unstructured data resembles a pile of magazines, newspapers and assorted papers scattered around the room. While each piece contains valuable information, locating a specific item amidst the chaos requires effort and specialized tools.

Structured data

Structured data is highly organized and easily searchable, typically stored in predefined formats such as tables with rows and columns. This organization makes it straightforward to input, query and analyse using tools like Microsoft Excel or SQL databases. For example, a company's sales records stored in an Excel spreadsheet might include rows representing individual transactions and columns detailing the date, customer ID, product ID, quantity sold and revenue generated. This clear structure allows analysts to quickly perform calculations, generate reports and identify trends without extensive preprocessing.

The advantages of structured data are significant. Its organized nature makes querying and analysis straightforward using standard tools, while consistent formatting reduces errors and discrepancies. Additionally, structured data can be efficiently stored and retrieved from databases, enabling quick access for decision-making. These features make structured data an invaluable asset for businesses looking to analyse and act on their information effectively.

Unstructured data

Unstructured data, unlike structured data, lacks a predefined format, making it more challenging to process and analyse. This type of data includes free text, multimedia content and other formats that do not fit neatly into tables or rows. For example, unstructured data might include emails, social media posts, PDFs, images, videos and audio files. These sources often contain valuable information, but extracting meaningful insights requires advanced techniques such as natural language processing (NLP) and machine learning algorithms.

Working with unstructured data presents several challenges. Its complexity demands sophisticated algorithms and substantial computational resources to extract relevant information.

Additionally, unstructured data is often large and varied, posing storage and management challenges. The lack of consistent formatting further complicates integration with structured datasets. While unstructured data holds immense potential, unlocking its value requires careful planning and advanced tools to overcome these obstacles.

Semi-structured data

Some data doesn't fit neatly into structured or unstructured categories. Semi-structured data combines elements of both, offering a hybrid format that balances the rigidity of structured data with the flexibility of unstructured data. For example, an email illustrates this blend: the header, containing sender, recipient and timestamp, is highly structured, while the body consists of free-form text. Similarly, formats like JSON and XML include structured tags and fields alongside flexible content, allowing for organization while accommodating variability.

This partially structured nature provides several advantages. Semi-structured data offers flexibility by handling diverse and evolving data types while retaining some level of organization. It integrates more easily with structured data compared to purely unstructured formats, making it a practical choice for many scenarios. Additionally, it is adaptable to situations where data formats may change over time, striking a balance between consistency and flexibility. This versatility makes semi-structured data an effective solution for managing complex and dynamic information.

Databases and data storage

While spreadsheets are great for small tasks, there comes a point when you need something more robust. Imagine running a growing business with thousands of customers and millions of transactions. Storing all that data in spreadsheets would be like trying to run a restaurant with only one stovetop burner; it might work at first, but it'll become unmanageable as you scale.

Databases are designed to handle large volumes of data efficiently and reliably. A database can store your information in a structured way, making it easier to update, search and analyse. With a database, you can ask complex questions like, 'What's the average engagement score for employees who've taken more than 10 hours of training?' and get answers quickly.

Most commonly, you'll encounter relational databases, which store data in tables, similar to spreadsheets but with added benefits like defined relationships between tables. This makes it simpler to combine information from different parts of your organization, such as linking employee performance records with training hours and department data. SQL is one of the most popular.

There are also non-relational (NoSQL) databases, better suited for unstructured or semi-structured data. These might store documents, images or logs that don't fit neatly into rows and columns. While relational databases are great for structured business data, NoSQL databases shine when handling more flexible, evolving data sources, such as social media comments or message logs between colleagues.

In addition to databases, organizations often use data warehouses for large-scale analytics. A data warehouse is like a high-capacity pantry, carefully stocked and organized so you can quickly find what you need to prepare any dish (analysis) you want. It's optimized for querying and reporting, enabling you to run complex analyses over historical data without slowing down day-to-day operations.

Ultimately, databases and data warehouses help you move beyond the limitations of spreadsheets. They ensure that as your data grows more complex and abundant, you can still manage it, ask meaningful questions and extract valuable insights efficiently and reliably.

Data silos

As you get more involved in working with data, especially if you work in a large company, you will start to encounter one of the biggest challenges in working with data: data silos. As the name suggests, a data silo is a collection of data that is only available to specific departments or individuals, even though it might be helpful to the whole organization. This happens when different departments, like HR, sales, finance, marketing, etc., each store and manage their data separately. This makes it a challenge for other departments to access and use that data. A typical scenario is for the marketing department to try to get access to sales data so they can see the impact of their marketing campaigns on sales, but the sales data is not accessible to them. It would benefit the business for the marketing team to be able to fine-tune their campaigns based on the resultant sales performance.

These data silos generally don't develop due to any malicious intent. They are usually the result of people taking their own initiative, without a central or governed approach, to gather the data they need for their role. While it might be a manageable situation for the people in that department, those in other departments might not even know it exists. What if the data is inaccurate, and is it being appropriately maintained according to company standards? One of the biggest challenges is that insights might be missed by not making this data available to the wider organization.

Breaking down data silos requires a company-wide approach and strategy. Though not always, they generally include having a centralized database or data warehouse that is governed and managed so that those with the necessary permissions can access what they need.

Quantitative versus qualitative data

As you grow more familiar with data sources and their formats, another clear distinction comes into play: the difference between quantitative and qualitative data. Just as structured, unstructured and semi-structured data shapes how you process information, whether your data is numeric or descriptive will guide the analysis techniques and interpretations you apply.

Quantitative data

Quantitative data is numerical and measurable. It answers questions like 'How many?', 'How much?' or 'How often?' and can be expressed as numbers, percentages, averages or other metrics. Think of sales figures that tell you the exact revenue made in a month, or engagement scores that show how frequently employees participate in a particular programme. Because quantitative data can be easily counted and compared, it lends itself well to statistical analysis, trend detection and performance measurement. For example, if your sales team sold 500 units last quarter, you can track if this number increases or decreases over time and correlate the changes with specific actions.

Qualitative data

Qualitative data, on the other hand, is descriptive rather than numeric. It focuses on the 'why' behind the numbers, capturing opinions, sentiments, experiences and motivations that are not easily reduced to figures or percentages. This type of data might come from open-ended survey responses, interviews with employees about their job satisfaction, customer reviews explaining what they love or dislike about a product, or social media posts reflecting brand perception. While qualitative data may feel more intangible, it offers depth and nuance. If your engagement scores (quantitative) are low in a specific department, qualitative feedback might reveal that employees feel undervalued or seek more career advancement opportunities. Without qualitative data, the underlying reasons for quantitative trends remain guesswork.

Balancing both types is typical for a comprehensive understanding. Quantitative data gives you a clear, objective snapshot of performance and outcomes, while qualitative data provides the rich context and human insights needed to interpret those results meaningfully. In practice, if your sales drop by 10 per cent (quantitative), conducting interviews or reading customer feedback (qualitative) might uncover that customers are unhappy with recent product changes. By combining both forms of data, you can make more informed decisions, adjusting product features, improving customer service or changing marketing messages to address issues revealed by the numbers and confirmed by people's voices.

Measures and dimensions

Two terms you will likely encounter early on, especially when working with dashboards and charts, are measures and dimensions. At first, these might sound like technical jargon, but think of them as two sides of a well-organized story: one side gives you the numbers and the other helps you understand what those numbers really mean.

Measures

Measures are all about quantity. They're the numeric values that you often want to sum, average or otherwise calculate to see how something is performing. For example, total sales revenue measures the number of products sold or the average employee engagement score. Measures are basically the answers to 'How much?' or 'How many?' and form the backbone of most performance metrics.

Dimensions

Dimensions, on the other hand, add the 'who,' 'what,' 'where' and 'when' to these numbers. If measures are the 'what happened' in your story, then dimensions explain 'in what context it happened'.

Dimensions categorize and organize your data so you can break down your measures into more meaningful views. For instance, instead of just knowing total sales revenue, you might use the dimension of 'Region' to see sales revenue by country or city. Or use the 'Department' dimension to understand employee engagement scores by team or function. By applying dimensions, you're effectively adding filters or categories that help you see patterns, pinpoint issues and find opportunities hidden within your numbers.

In simple terms, measures are the raw numbers you care about, while dimensions give those numbers a place, a category or a timeframe. Together, they allow you to transform a jumble of values into a clear, insightful picture of what's going on in your business.

Table 5.1 Measures and dimensions

Employee ID	Department	Supervisor rating	Promotions	Engagement score
001	Sales	4	1	85%
002	Marketing	3	0	72%
003	Sales	5	2	60%

- Measures: Supervisor rating, promotions, engagement score
- Dimensions: Department, employee ID

Example

Let's continue with the HR analytics scenario. Your refined question is: 'What career development initiatives can we implement for the software development team to reduce turnover by 10 per cent within the next six months?'

In this chapter, your focus will be on understanding the data sources and data types that will help you address this question.

Before diving into analysis, it's essential to build a strong foundation by identifying and categorizing your data sources, distinguishing between types of data and understanding how measures and dimensions will structure your insights.

Step 1: Identify and categorize your data sources

Begin by identifying the data sources you'll need to address the question. Organize these sources as internal or external and categorize them by format: structured, semi-structured or unstructured. This helps you understand what tools and processes you'll need to handle the data.

Internal data sources:

- **HRIS (human resource information system):** Provides structured data such as promotions, training history and turnover rates.

- **Engagement surveys:** Semi-structured data with numeric scores and open-ended responses.

- **Exit interview records:** Unstructured data in free-text format that captures employee feedback.

External data sources:

- **Industry retention reports:** Semi-structured benchmarks comparing your turnover rates to industry standards.

- **Job review platforms:** Unstructured qualitative data from employee reviews on sites like Glassdoor or Indeed.

By categorizing these sources, you'll prepare yourself for gathering the right data efficiently and avoid missing critical information.

Step 2: Understand types of data

Each data source contains different types of data that require specific approaches for processing and interpretation. Recognizing whether your data is structured, unstructured or semi-structured will guide how you manage and prepare it:

- **Structured data**
  This includes well-organized formats like tables from HRIS systems, where rows and columns represent specific attributes, such as employee tenure or training hours.

- **Unstructured data**
  Examples include text from exit interviews or social media reviews. This data is not easily organized into tables and requires more advanced tools to process, such as natural language processing (NLP).

- **Semi-structured data**
  Sources like engagement surveys or JSON files combine structured elements (e.g. survey scores) with unstructured elements (e.g. open-ended feedback).

Understanding these distinctions ensures you'll be ready to handle and integrate data from diverse formats.

Step 3: Balance quantitative and qualitative data

Your data will fall into two broad categories: quantitative and qualitative. Both are essential for a complete understanding of the problem:

- **Quantitative data (the 'what')**
  Metrics like turnover rates, average engagement scores or the number of training hours per employee. These are numeric and measurable.

- **Qualitative data (the 'why')**
  Descriptive data from exit interviews or employee reviews that capture opinions and experiences. This helps uncover the reasons behind the quantitative trends.

Balancing these two types of data ensures you'll have both a clear picture of what's happening and context to interpret it later.

Step 4: Identify measures and dimensions

To structure your data for analysis, think in terms of measures and dimensions:

- **Measures:** Numeric values you'll track, such as:
  - o Turnover rate (% of employees leaving within a specific timeframe)
  - o Average engagement score
  - o Training hours per developer
- **Dimensions:** Categories that provide context to measures, such as:
  - o Department (e.g. software development)
  - o Tenure (e.g. 0–2 years, 3–5 years)
  - o Engagement segments (e.g. high vs. low scorers)

By defining measures and dimensions upfront, you'll be able to organize your data into actionable components for analysis.

Step 5: Address data silos

As you gather data, you might encounter silos – data stored separately in different systems or departments. For example, training records might be managed by the Learning and Development team, while turnover data is in HRIS. These silos can limit your ability to get a complete view.

Solution:

Start by identifying where data silos exist and collaborating with relevant teams to centralize the data. For example:

- work with the learning and development team to access training records;
- align data formats and ensure proper permissions are in place for seamless integration.

Breaking down silos early will save time and prevent roadblocks in later stages.

By following these steps, you've built a clear map of your data landscape. At this stage, you're not analysing or interpreting the data yet. Instead, you're laying the groundwork for efficient and accurate data management by:

- categorizing data sources (internal vs. external) and types (structured, semi-structured, unstructured);

- balancing quantitative and qualitative data to capture both metrics and context;

- structuring your data with measures and dimensions to create a framework for future analysis;

- addressing potential silos to ensure smooth data integration.

This foundation will ensure that when you're ready to move into analysis, you'll have everything you need to work confidently and effectively.

Exercise

1 **Identify data characteristics**
Consider a hypothetical dataset related to your organization or a familiar scenario. List three data sources you might use (e.g. sales records, customer feedback forms, industry reports). For each source, identify:

   o whether it is internal or external

   o whether it's structured, semi-structured or unstructured

   o a measure you might derive from it (e.g. sales revenue, number of training hours)

   o a dimension that would help provide context (e.g. region, department, month).

2 **Categorize data types**
Take a quantitative metric you're familiar with (like average product rating or employee turnover rate) and brainstorm one qualitative source that could help explain the 'why' behind that number (e.g. customer comments, employee exit interviews). How would this combination help you make better decisions?

3 **Reflect on metadata**

For one of your chosen data sources, imagine you are creating metadata. Write a short description that includes:

o the data source origin (e.g. 'sales CRM system')

o the date or frequency of updates

o who maintains it

o the format (e.g. CSV, Excel, JSON)

Explain how this metadata entry would help another analyst who is new to the dataset.

Summary points

- **Know your sources**
  Understanding whether data comes from inside or outside your organization helps set realistic expectations about relevance, control and integration challenges.

- **Recognize data formats**
  Structured, unstructured, and semi-structured data each have unique implications for how you'll store, process and analyse information.

- **Balance quantitative and qualitative**
  Numbers tell you what's happening, but words and stories reveal why.

- **Use measures and dimensions wisely**
  Measures give you the raw metrics, while dimensions provide the context that turns raw numbers into insights.

- **Metadata is your guide**
  Treat metadata as the catalogue that keeps your data collections navigable, understandable and reliable.

06

Navigating data privacy and ethics

A cautionary tale

In 2018, the world witnessed one of the most high-profile data privacy breaches in history: the Cambridge Analytica scandal. This political consulting firm accessed personal data from millions of Facebook users without their explicit consent, leveraging the information to create psychological profiles and target individuals with political advertisements. The fallout was immense. Facebook faced a record-breaking $5 billion fine from the Federal Trade Commission, and the scandal damaged public trust in social media platforms and data-driven advertising.

The Cambridge Analytica case is a stark reminder of the risks tied to irresponsible data handling. Beyond legal consequences, organizations can suffer severe reputational harm, customer distrust and loss of stakeholder confidence. It highlights the need to treat data privacy and ethics as fundamental to any organization's data practices, not just to avoid penalties but to maintain credibility and foster trust.

This chapter explores how to approach data responsibly, addressing key privacy regulations like GDPR and CCPA, as well as the importance of ethical considerations in data use. By understanding the principles of data privacy and governance, you'll be equipped to manage data in a way that respects individual rights, adheres to legal standards and strengthens your organization's reputation.

Understanding data privacy

At its core, data privacy revolves around the idea that certain information should be protected, especially details that can identify a person or reveal something sensitive about them. Personal data generally includes information like names, email addresses, home addresses or identification numbers. Sensitive data is even more delicate, often covering things like health records, financial details, racial or ethnic origin, religious beliefs or sexual orientation. The key point is that this data can affect a person's life if misused or exposed without consent.

In many regions, a commonly used term is PII (Personally Identifiable Information), which refers to any data that could be used to identify a specific individual. PII often includes details like social security numbers, passport numbers, phone numbers or any unique combination of attributes that can pinpoint a person. Recognizing PII helps organizations to know when to apply stricter safeguards.

In the healthcare sector, HIPAA (Health Insurance Portability and Accountability Act) in the United States sets the standard for protecting sensitive patient health information. Under HIPAA, health-related personal data must be handled with heightened care to maintain confidentiality, ensure integrity and prevent unauthorized access. Even if your work isn't strictly in healthcare, understanding HIPAA exemplifies the importance of sector-specific regulations that add extra layers of responsibility when handling especially sensitive information.

Data privacy isn't just about following rules but respecting individuals. When employees, customers or stakeholders share their information with your organization, they are placing trust in you. Upholding that trust by keeping their data safe and using it responsibly enhances your organization's credibility and reputation. On the legal side, various laws require you to handle personal and sensitive data carefully, so respecting privacy also means staying compliant and avoiding hefty penalties.

When privacy is compromised, say through a data breach, your organization can face serious consequences. Financially, you might be hit with hefty fines. Operationally, you could be forced to halt certain activities to fix the problem. From a reputation standpoint, you risk losing the trust you've worked hard to build. Customers and employees may take their business and talent elsewhere, and negative headlines can linger in the public consciousness for a long time. In short, protecting personal and sensitive data, including PII and any data covered under specialized regulations like HIPAA, is not just a moral obligation, it's a sound business strategy and a cornerstone of ethical data management.

Key regulations

To help ensure data privacy isn't left up to interpretation alone, governments have introduced regulations that set standards for how personal data should be handled. Two prominent examples are the GDPR (General Data Protection Regulation) in the European Union and the CCPA (California Consumer Privacy Act) in the United States.

GDPR (General Data Protection Regulation)

The GDPR was established in the European Union to protect the personal data of EU citizens, regardless of where that data is stored or processed. This means that even companies outside of Europe must comply if they handle data belonging to EU citizens.

Key principles of GDPR include obtaining explicit and informed consent before collecting personal data. It also grants individuals the 'right to be forgotten', allowing them to request the deletion of their personal data when it is no longer necessary. Additionally,

GDPR emphasizes data minimization, requiring organizations to collect and store only the data that is strictly necessary, thereby reducing unnecessary exposure. These principles collectively aim to enhance data privacy and ensure responsible data management.

CCPA (California Consumer Privacy Act)

The California Consumer Privacy Act (CCPA) governs how businesses handle the personal information of California residents. While its scope is localized, its impact extends nationwide, as many companies serve customers in California.

CCPA grants individuals key rights, including the right to disclosure, which requires companies to inform individuals about the personal data they collect and how it is used. It also allows individuals to opt out of the sale of their personal information, giving them greater control over how their data is shared.

Though GDPR and CCPA are region-specific, their core message is universal: individuals have the right to understand how their data is used and to maintain control over it. These regulations emphasize respect, transparency and accountability, forming the foundation of responsible data practices globally.

Ethical considerations in data handling

Compliance with the law is essential, but ethical behaviour requires going a step further. Ethics involves doing what's right, even when no one is watching, by using data in ways that are respectful, fair and beneficial rather than exploitative. Just because a particular use of data isn't explicitly prohibited by regulations doesn't mean it's ethically sound. For instance, while you may have legal permission to use customer data for marketing, bombarding individuals with invasive targeted ads could erode trust and create discomfort. Legally permissible actions can still carry ethical consequences.

Ethical data use is guided by principles such as honesty, fairness and transparency. Being honest means clearly explaining why you're collecting data and how it will be used. Fairness ensures that data practices do not disadvantage any group or individual. Transparency involves openly communicating data usage policies and any changes, empowering people to make informed choices.

Unethical practices, such as creating discriminatory hiring algorithms or using customer data for unauthorized purposes, risk not only regulatory penalties but also significant harm to individuals and your organization's reputation. Selling personal information to third parties without consent is another clear example of behaviour that undermines trust and ethical standards.

By prioritizing ethical data handling, you move beyond merely meeting legal requirements to fostering a culture of responsibility and respect. This approach strengthens relationships with employees, customers and the broader public, creating long-term trust and credibility.

Anonymization and minimizing personal identifiers

As you strive to protect individuals' identities and respect their privacy, you may find that you don't always need detailed personal information to achieve your analytical goals. Anonymization is the process of removing or modifying personal identifiers so that data can no longer be traced back to specific individuals. This can be done in several ways.

Masking replaces personal identifiers, such as names or ID numbers, with pseudonyms or random strings. For example, 'Jane Smith' could become 'Employee A002'. Aggregation involves grouping data at a higher level to obscure individual details, for instance, analysing average salaries by department rather than examining each employee's pay. Suppression removes specific fields entirely when they are unnecessary, such as stripping out home addresses if regional data suffices.

While anonymization is crucial for privacy protection, it's important to maintain the utility of the data. Over-suppressing or aggregating can dilute the insights you can derive. The goal is to strike a balance where personal identifiers are effectively removed, yet the data's trends and patterns remain clear.

Anonymization not only helps you comply with regulations like GDPR and CCPA, since anonymized data often falls outside their stricter rules, but also aligns with ethical standards by respecting individuals' rights. By handling data responsibly in this way, you foster trust and enable analysis and innovation without breaching ethical or legal boundaries.

Data governance basics

As your organization grows and more people interact with data, keeping track of responsibilities can become challenging. Data governance provides a structured framework to ensure that data is well managed, reliable and consistently handled according to established standards.

Governance addresses key questions such as: Who owns the data and makes decisions about its use? Who are the stewards responsible for maintaining its quality and ensuring compliance? What rules and standards dictate how data is stored, accessed and shared? These roles and policies create clarity and accountability, ensuring data is handled responsibly.

Effective governance doesn't require a complex bureaucracy. Simple steps can make a big difference, such as assigning data owners for major datasets to ensure clear points of contact for resolving issues. Documenting data handling policies, including update schedules, approval processes for changes and retention guidelines, provides structure and consistency. Setting clear retention periods prevents data from being kept longer than necessary, reducing both risk and unnecessary clutter.

With governance in place, proving compliance during audits becomes easier and stakeholders gain confidence in your data practices. Beyond regulatory compliance, strong governance prevents errors like accidental data exposure or inconsistent definitions, maintaining trust both within the organization and with external partners.

Access permissions and controls

Even with careful planning, ethical guidelines and anonymization, a fundamental question remains: Who gets to see what data? Not everyone in an organization needs to view sensitive information, and some data, especially personal or confidential details, should be tightly restricted. This is where access permissions and controls come into play.

Access controls ensure that individuals only handle the data they legitimately need. For instance, a payroll specialist might have the right to view salary records but a marketing analyst typically does not. By clearly defining which roles can access sensitive fields, organizations reduce the risk of accidental misuse and safeguard personal information from unnecessary exposure.

Role-based access

In practice, access is often granted based on an employee's job function or role. Systems might assign predefined permissions to roles like 'HR Manager' or 'Data Analyst,' rather than to specific people. When someone changes roles, their permissions can be updated without a complicated overhaul. This approach not only streamlines access management but also helps maintain consistent and fair rules across the organization.

Accountability and transparency

Robust permission systems usually include auditing features that track who viewed or modified data and when. This audit trail is vital if there's ever a suspicion of improper access or a data leak;

it allows the organization to pinpoint when and how an issue occurred and address it promptly. Regular audits and reviews of access logs also encourage everyone to respect and follow the established rules.

When employees understand their boundaries, knowing what data they can access and what's off limits, they're less likely to stumble into sensitive areas accidentally. This clarity helps prevent well-intentioned but uninformed team members from breaching privacy or compliance standards.

Working within the system

As someone working with data, you might not control these permissions yourself, but understanding their purpose helps you navigate the data landscape more confidently. If you need certain information, you'll know why it might not be directly visible and can collaborate with data owners or IT teams to request appropriate levels of access. Conversely, if you handle sensitive data, you'll appreciate the checks and balances that protect both the organization and the individuals the data represents.

One of the most common challenges in data acquisition is that access approval can take time, especially when crossing departmental boundaries. To prevent delays, reach out to data custodians or system administrators early in the process. These individuals are often responsible for managing access to specific data sources and they can clarify any prerequisites, permissions and protocols. By notifying them in advance, you allow them time to process your request, which is especially helpful if they need to coordinate with IT or security teams for access.

Providing advance notice also gives you the chance to explain why you need the data and how it aligns with your business objectives. Data owners and custodians are more likely to support your request when they understand the context and purpose. When possible, connect your data needs back to broader organizational goals, showing them how your work will contribute to success across the organization.

By embracing access controls, organizations strike a balance between data utility and privacy protection. For you, it means a safer, more transparent environment where data-driven insights can flourish responsibly.

Example

In this chapter, you're focusing on ensuring that your data-handling practices are both ethical and compliant with data privacy regulations. Before diving into analysis, it's important to prepare your data responsibly by applying anonymization techniques, setting access permissions and establishing governance. This ensures you're protecting employee privacy while laying the groundwork for meaningful insights later.

Step 1: Identify sensitive fields

Begin by reviewing your datasets to pinpoint which fields might include personally identifiable information (PII) or sensitive data. In the HR context, this might include:

- employee names
- supervisor comments from engagement surveys
- specific feedback in exit interviews
- salary and compensation details

Recognizing sensitive fields helps you determine what needs extra protection to comply with privacy laws like GDPR or CCPA and to uphold ethical standards.

Step 2: Apply anonymization

Before proceeding with data preparation, anonymize sensitive fields to protect individual identities while retaining the utility of the data for analysis. For example:

- **Masking:** Replace employee names with pseudonyms or random IDs (e.g. 'Jane Smith' becomes 'Employee A002').

- **Aggregation:** Instead of showing individual salaries, use group data to show average salaries by department.
- **Suppression:** Remove unnecessary sensitive fields, such as home addresses, if the data is not relevant to your analysis.

By applying these techniques, you ensure that your data is compliant with privacy regulations and less vulnerable to misuse.

Step 3: Establish governance and ownership

Clear governance ensures that data is managed responsibly. For this scenario:

- **Data ownership:** Designate the head of HR as the data owner for employee records. They have ultimate accountability for decisions about how the data is used.

- **Data stewardship:** Assign an HR analyst as the data steward to oversee the daily management of the data, such as maintaining its accuracy and ensuring compliance with privacy policies.

Documenting these roles ensures there is accountability and clarity about who is responsible for safeguarding the data.

Step 4: Set access controls

Not everyone in your organization needs to access sensitive employee data. Use role-based access controls to limit who can see what:

- **HR managers:** Can access individual-level data, such as engagement scores and detailed feedback, to design targeted initiatives.

- **Marketing analysts:** Can only see aggregated results, like department-level trends, to ensure they do not access private employee information.

- **IT teams:** Have limited access to ensure systems are functioning but cannot view sensitive employee details.

This ensures sensitive data is only accessible to those who genuinely need it, reducing the risk of accidental exposure or misuse.

Step 5: Transparency and documentation

Finally, ensure your approach to data handling is transparent and well documented. For example:

- **Policies:** Create a written policy that outlines how employee data is anonymized, who can access it and how it will be used.

- **Audit trails:** Use system logs to track who accesses sensitive data and when, ensuring accountability.

- **Communications:** Inform employees that their data is anonymized and handled responsibly, reinforcing trust.

By being transparent about your processes, you demonstrate ethical data practices and build confidence among employees and stakeholders.

By taking these steps, you've ensured that your data handling practices align with privacy regulations and ethical standards. Although you're not analysing the data yet, your preparation ensures that:

- sensitive fields are protected through anonymization

- data access is controlled to reduce risks of misuse

- governance roles are in place to maintain accountability

- your organization is compliant with regulations like GDPR and CCPA

These precautions create a solid foundation for future analysis while upholding employee trust and safeguarding personal information.

In the next chapter, you'll dive into cleaning and organizing this data for actionable insights. For now, focus on refining your approach to responsible data handling – it's the cornerstone of ethical and effective analytics.

Exercise

You are tasked with analysing customer feedback and purchase history at an online retailer. Customer feedback often includes personal details and may reference specific complaints about service representatives.

1 **Identify sensitive fields**
   Which parts of your data might directly identify customers or employees?

2 **Propose anonymization techniques**
   How would you mask or aggregate data to keep personal details hidden while still extracting insights?

3 **Set access permissions**
   Consider who should have full access, who needs aggregated views and who shouldn't see certain fields at all.

4 **List one governance measure**
   Pick a simple governance action, like assigning a data owner for customer data, and explain how it helps maintain trust and compliance.

Summary points

- **Privacy is paramount**
  Protecting personal data is not just about legal compliance; it's about respecting individuals and maintaining their trust.

- **Ethics extend beyond the law**
  Legal standards provide a baseline, but ethical considerations push you to do what's right, strengthening relationships and reputation.

- **Governance and control aid compliance**
  By establishing clear roles, policies and permissions, you create a culture of responsibility and reduce the risk of breaches or misuse.

- **Anonymization is a powerful tool**
  Removing personal identifiers lets you preserve data utility while protecting people's privacy, aligning with both regulations and ethical standards.

- **Small steps, big impact**
  Documenting sensitive fields, offering regular training and revisiting policies periodically all contribute to a sustainable, trustworthy data environment.

Part 4
Preparing and integrating data

07

Extracting and preparing data

Assembling the ingredients

Imagine you're preparing a meal for a group of guests. Before you can start cooking, you need to gather the right ingredients from various sources: the pantry, the refrigerator and perhaps a quick trip to the store. Some ingredients might require prep – washing, peeling or chopping – before they're ready to use. Just like cooking a meal requires the right ingredients prepared in the right way, data analysis depends on extracting the correct data and transforming it into a usable format.

Data extraction and transformation work similarly. Before diving into analysis, data must first be 'unpacked' from various sources and shapes, then 'tuned up' to ensure it's consistent, clean and ready for use. This chapter focuses on the 'Extract' step highlighted in the BRICE framework, turning raw, scattered data into a well-prepared resource you can trust.

Building on what you learned about data sources and types in Chapter 5 and recalling the importance of privacy and governance from Chapter 6, this chapter explores the practical steps of retrieving data and making it suitable for meaningful insight. Just as a successful meal requires careful preparation of the ingredients, practical data analysis hinges on proper extraction and transformation. By the end of this chapter, you'll have the know-how to ensure your data is both accessible and analysis-ready, paving the way for smarter, more reliable decisions.

The role of extraction in the data pipeline

Before you can analyse, visualize or derive insights from data, it needs to be retrieved and organized, a process known as extraction. In the commonly used ETL (Extract, Transform, Load) process, extraction is the first step. It involves pulling data from various systems, databases or files and preparing it for further processing. Think of this stage as collecting all your ingredients from the pantry, fridge and store before you start cooking.

Extract

This step involves retrieving data from one or more sources. These sources could be structured, such as relational databases or spreadsheets, or unstructured, like text files, social media data or email logs. The extracted data is raw and may come in various formats or levels of completeness, making it essential to capture everything relevant for the analysis that follows.

Transform

After extracting the data, it must be cleaned and transformed into a format suitable for analysis. This process ensures the data is accurate, consistent and ready for use, much like preparing ingredients in a kitchen before cooking. Key steps include removing duplicates to avoid inaccuracies, addressing missing or NULL values by imputing, flagging or excluding them based on the context, and converting data types, such as transforming text-based dates into proper date formats.

Other important transformations include aggregating data, such as calculating total hours worked by employees or summarizing sales by region, and standardizing formats, like ensuring all salary data is in the same currency or timestamps reflect consistent time zones. These steps are essential for creating a reliable dataset.

Skipping this stage risks introducing errors, leading to misleading or incomplete insights. Data cleaning and transformation lay the foundation for effective and accurate analysis.

Load

After the data has been transformed, it is ready to be loaded into a target system. This could be a database, a data warehouse or an analytical tool such as Power BI or Tableau. The load process ensures that the prepared data is accessible, organized and primed for analysis. Think of this as plating and serving a well-prepared meal to your guests. The quality and readiness of the data at this stage directly impact the ease and reliability of the subsequent analysis.

ETL vs ELT

While ETL is a familiar acronym (Extract, Transform, Load) some organizations follow a slightly different sequence known as ELT (Extract, Load, Transform). In ELT, you first extract the raw data and load it 'as is' into a storage system (such as a data lake) and then transform it as needed. ELT can offer greater flexibility when dealing with big data or complex data landscapes, but ETL remains a solid and straightforward choice for many standard use cases. In either approach, extraction sets the stage by ensuring you have all the relevant data on hand, ready for whatever transformations come next.

In Chapter 5, you explored internal and external data sources as well as different data formats (structured, semi-structured and unstructured). This knowledge now becomes crucial. Extracting data from an internal relational database might be as simple as running an SQL query, while pulling data from an external API may require understanding authentication methods, rate limits and response formats. Unstructured data, like logs or social media posts, might need specialized scripts or tools to parse. Recognizing these differences allows you to choose the appropriate extraction method and handle each source's quirks effectively.

Data extraction techniques

Now that you understand the significance of extraction and the challenges that might arise, let's consider some common techniques and strategies. While you don't need to become an expert in every method, familiarizing yourself with these approaches will help you identify the best fit for your data and environment.

Querying databases

For structured, internal data, like customer transactions or employee records, relational databases are often the starting point. You can use a language called SQL (Structured Query Language) to extract precisely the records and fields you need. Tools such as ODBC or JDBC drivers let you connect to databases from various applications, ensuring a smooth path to retrieve data. Think of it like placing a special order at a restaurant: you specify exactly what you want and the kitchen (database) returns just that, saving time and effort.

APIs and web services

External sources often provide data through APIs (Application Programming Interfaces), basically, convenient 'doors' you can knock on to request specific information. For example, a weather API might let you retrieve today's forecast, or a social media API might return recent posts about your product. While APIs are handy, you must respect their rules (rate limits that cap how many requests you can make and authentication tokens that prove you have permission). Handling these constraints is like working with a polite but busy librarian; you can borrow materials, but only so many at once, and you need the proper library card.

Web scraping

Sometimes the data you need isn't offered in a structured format or via an API. Web scraping involves programmatically reading web pages and extracting useful information. For instance, you might scrape prices from a competitor's website. However, web scraping comes with ethical and legal considerations. Some websites prohibit it outright, and even when allowed, you should be gentle; sending too many automated requests can overwhelm the site. Always check terms of service and be respectful, just as you would when visiting someone's home.

Full vs incremental extraction

When determining how much data to extract, there are two primary approaches to consider. Full extraction involves pulling all available data each time. While this method is straightforward, it can be slow and inefficient, especially for large datasets. In contrast, incremental extraction retrieves only new or modified records since the last extraction, making it more efficient and ensuring smoother processes by avoiding unnecessary reprocessing.

Think of it like a weekly grocery run: full extraction is akin to buying every single item from your pantry each week, whether you need it or not, which is wasteful and time-consuming. Incremental extraction, however, is like restocking only the items you've run out of since your last trip, saving time and resources.

You don't need to master these techniques in detail, but understanding the difference allows you to choose the approach that best suits your evolving data needs. With this knowledge, you can gather data more efficiently, laying a strong foundation for the transformative steps that follow.

Data transformation

Extraction provides raw data, but raw doesn't always mean ready. Just as freshly harvested vegetables need peeling, chopping and seasoning before becoming part of a dish, data transformation refines, reorganizes and enhances extracted data to make it consistent, reliable and useful for analysis.

Data transformation involves adjusting raw data into a cleaner, more uniform state. The process resolves inconsistencies, fills gaps and ensures that the data is ready for meaningful analysis. Think of it as a quality control step, ensuring that analytical techniques, whether simple calculations or advanced algorithms – yield accurate results without being skewed by messy inputs.

The transformation process begins with cleaning, where issues such as missing values, typos and duplicates are addressed. This might involve removing incomplete rows, replacing empty cells with default values or standardizing inconsistencies, such as unifying records that use 'US' and 'USA' into a single format. Next comes formatting, which ensures that diverse data forms are standardized. For instance, dates written as '2021-07-10' and 'July 10, 2021' are aligned into a consistent pattern, text-based numbers are converted to numeric values and units of measurement are made uniform.

Aggregation is another important step, where detailed data is summarized into higher-level insights. Instead of analysing thousands of individual sales transactions, you might aggregate monthly sales totals by product line, making it easier to identify trends and patterns. Finally, enrichment adds context to your data by incorporating supplemental information. For example, merging employee productivity data with department details or attaching regional economic indicators to sales data can provide deeper insights.

Through these steps, data transformation refines raw information into a polished, structured format, ensuring that it is both accurate and actionable. This careful preparation sets the foundation for reliable analysis and meaningful insights.

Data quality

No matter how well you plan your data extraction or how skill-fully you transform your data, if the end result isn't accurate or reliable, your analysis will suffer. Data quality is the cornerstone of meaningful insights. Think of it like choosing fresh, well-grown produce for your meal; no amount of skilled cooking can save a dish made from spoiled ingredients.

Don't wait until the very end to check your data's quality. As you extract and transform, keep an eye out for problems. Are there missing values in critical fields? Do some records contain strange or impossible entries, like negative ages or future dates that don't make sense? Spotting these issues early lets you fix them before they throw off your analysis.

As you clean, reformat or merge data, note what you did and why. This doesn't have to be complicated; just a brief log in a document or a few comments in a script can help you (and others) remember what changes were made. Documentation makes it easier to retrace your steps if something goes wrong or if you need to explain your methods to a colleague down the road.

It's tempting to streamline your extraction and transformation processes for speed, but be careful not to sacrifice quality. Sometimes, taking an extra moment to review a strange-looking record or verify a source's reliability is worth the slight delay. Just as rushing through meal prep could lead to a mishap in the kitchen, rushing through data prep can lead to faulty conclusions.

Data extraction and transformation rarely come out perfect on the first try. Start with a simple approach, learn from what worked and what didn't, and refine your process in future iterations. Maybe you'll discover a better way to handle missing values, or perhaps a more efficient order of steps reduces the chance of errors. Each round of improvement raises the bar for data quality.

By centring your efforts on maintaining data quality throughout extraction and transformation, you ensure that the insights you draw are built on a solid foundation. Over time, these best practices will become second nature, making your data projects smoother, more reliable and ultimately more valuable.

Common challenges

Despite careful planning, extracting and transforming data often presents real-world challenges that require thoughtful strategies to overcome. Large datasets, for instance, can make traditional methods impractical. Breaking data into smaller batches, using streaming techniques or leveraging specialized tools like cloud platforms for high-volume processing can address these issues. Starting with a test subset before scaling up ensures efficiency and reliability.

Missing fields or incomplete data are common hurdles. Decisions must be made about whether to skip incomplete rows, fill gaps with default values or flag them for review. Similarly, unstructured formats like text files or PDFs, or incompatible formats such as JSON files requiring conversion to CSV, often necessitate advanced parsing or preprocessing tools.

Rate limits and restricted access, particularly with external APIs, can slow extraction. Incremental pulls or off-peak scheduling can help, as can aligning extraction schedules with the varying update cycles of different data sources. Some systems refresh data daily, while others do so weekly, making timing crucial to ensure the most accurate snapshot is used.

By anticipating these challenges, whether dealing with scale, incomplete data, unstructured formats or access limitations, you can adapt your processes to maintain smooth data pipelines. These preparations ensure your extracted and transformed data is both reliable and ready for meaningful analysis, even under less-than-ideal conditions.

Example

Continuing with the HR analytics scenario, your focus shifts to preparing the data necessary to explore the relationship between training participation and employee engagement. Previously, you identified training hours and engagement survey results as key metrics for this analysis. In this chapter, you'll concentrate on extracting the data from various internal systems and transforming it into a clean, consistent and analysis-ready format.

Step 1: Extraction

The first step involves gathering data from different systems:

- **HR system:** You query the HR database to extract employee details, their department and total training hours completed in the past 12 months. Using an SQL query, you specify filters to retrieve only employees in the software development department to keep your scope aligned with the original question. The query returns fields such as Employee_ID, Training_Hours and Department.

- **Engagement survey platform:** Engagement data is retrieved via the platform's API, which returns survey results in JSON format. The data includes fields like Employee_ID, Engagement_Score and Survey_Date. However, the JSON format requires additional work to integrate with the tabular data from the HR system.

You now have two datasets in different formats – one from the HR system (structured and tabular) and one from the survey platform (semi-structured JSON).

Step 2: Transformation

With the extracted data in hand, the next step is transforming it into a unified and consistent structure.

- **Clean the engagement survey data**
  - Convert all Engagement_Score values into a numeric format to ensure they're suitable for calculations.
  - Remove any rows missing an Employee_ID to avoid inconsistencies during the merge.
  - Standardize the Survey_Date field to follow a common format (e.g. YYYY-MM-DD).

- **Aggregate engagement scores**
  - Some employees participated in multiple surveys throughout the year. To simplify the data, calculate the average Engagement_Score for each employee. This provides a single representative score per individual, making the dataset more manageable.

- **Enrich the data**
  - Merge the cleaned and aggregated survey data with the HR system data using Employee_ID as the common key. This results in a combined dataset that includes Employee_ID, Department, Training_Hours, and Average_Engagement_Score for each employee in the software development department.

Step 3: Ensuring data quality and privacy

As part of your transformation process, you validate the data and ensure it adheres to privacy and governance standards:

- **Validation**
  - Check for duplicates and ensure that each Employee_ID appears only once in the final dataset.
  - Spot-check data for inconsistencies, such as negative training hours or engagement scores outside the expected range (e.g. 0–100).

- **Privacy protections**
  - o Remove unnecessary fields like employee names or other personal identifiers, focusing only on the metrics required for the analysis.
  - o Mask or pseudonymize Employee_ID if it's not needed for the analysis.

- **Documentation**
  - o Record each step of the extraction and transformation process, including the SQL queries, the method used to clean and aggregate engagement scores, and any assumptions made along the way. This ensures transparency and replicability.

By the end of this process, you have a clean, unified dataset that is ready for analysis. This dataset includes:

- total training hours completed by each software developer in the past year;

- their average engagement score based on survey results.

At this stage, you've set the foundation for examining whether a relationship exists between training participation and engagement. You haven't conducted the analysis yet, but your well-prepared data ensures the upcoming steps will yield reliable and meaningful insights.

Exercise

Take a basic CSV file and imagine it's a set of employee timesheets with columns for Employee ID, Date and Hours Worked. Outline the steps you'd use to prepare this data for a productivity analysis:

1 **Extraction:** This is already done if you have the CSV, but imagine you might have needed to download it from an internal portal.

2 **Cleaning:** Are there any rows with missing Hours? Decide how to handle them (filling with 0 or removing them).

3 **Formatting:** Ensure all dates follow the same format and Hours are numeric (not text).

4 **Aggregating:** Summarize total hours per employee per month.

5 **Documentation:** Write down what you changed and why so you or your colleagues can understand and repeat the process later if needed.

By working through this exercise, you put into practice the concepts of extracting raw data and turning it into a structured, analysis-ready format.

Summary points

- **Extraction sets the foundation**
  Pulling data from various sources at the right time and in a manageable format is the first step to gaining meaningful insights. Without careful extraction, no amount of analysis will yield dependable results.

- **Transformation makes data useful**
  By cleaning, standardizing and enriching your extracted data, you turn a jumble of raw information into something coherent and actionable. Transformation ensures consistency and clarity, making it easier to spot trends and answer the questions that matter.

- **Quality and clarity matter at every stage**
  Extraction and transformation aren't just technical chores; they're about ensuring data quality. Documenting your processes, validating your data and improving your methods over time all contribute to more reliable outcomes and more productive work downstream.

08

Integrating data

The sum of the whole

Picture yourself putting together the final dish after carefully gathering and preparing your ingredients. You've sourced them (extraction), cleaned and chopped them (transformation) and now it's time to combine these components into a cohesive meal. In the data world, this step is called integration, merging multiple datasets into a single, unified resource that tells a richer, more complete story.

Up to this point, you've learned where to find data, how to clean and shape it and how to ensure it respects privacy and ethical standards. Now you'll move beyond treating each dataset as a stand-alone element and start blending them together. By establishing common keys (like a shared Employee_ID) and choosing the right kind of join (e.g. inner, left or full outer), you can weave different data sources into one seamless dataset.

This chapter will guide you through the concepts and best practices of data integration. We'll explore how to identify the right fields to link datasets, ensure data quality during the merge and document your choices, perhaps by maintaining a simple data dictionary for clarity. As you integrate engagement surveys, training hours, department rosters and external benchmarks, you'll gain a more holistic perspective than any single dataset could provide on its own.

By the end, you'll not only understand how to connect the dots between various data sources but also be able to apply this skill to any analytics project. Integration transforms a scattered collection of ingredients into a harmonious, insight-filled feast for the mind.

Why data integration is important

If each dataset you've extracted and transformed is like a single musical instrument playing its own tune, integrated data is the full orchestra playing a well-coordinated symphony. Without integration, you might be stuck listening to individual instruments without ever hearing the complete harmony.

In many organizations, data lives in separate 'silos': HR records in one database, training logs in another, engagement surveys in a spreadsheet and market benchmarks on a separate platform. On their own, these fragments tell part of the story but leave critical gaps. By integrating these sources, you unify previously isolated datasets, allowing them to complement each other. Think of it as opening the doors between separate rooms so everyone can share what they know, revealing a more holistic understanding of the issues at hand.

When you combine data, you can uncover relationships you couldn't see before. For instance, tying together training hours, engagement scores and turnover rates might reveal that employees who invest in professional development are not just more skilled, they're also more engaged and less likely to leave. Adding external data, like industry benchmarks, can show whether your retention efforts are on par with competitors. Integration transforms separate clues into a clearer picture, enabling more targeted decision-making.

Without integration, you risk having multiple 'versions' of what you consider factual; different reports might show slightly different numbers for the same metric because they rely on different datasets or calculation methods. When data is integrated, everyone in the organization references the same source, minimizing confusion and inconsistency. This shared foundation ensures more credible analyses and smoother collaboration across teams.

In short, integration moves you from piecemeal observations to rich, contextual insights that drive informed actions. It's a pivotal step that brings your data strategy full circle, ensuring your analysis rests on a comprehensive and reliable base.

Keys, relationships and consistency

Integrating data from multiple sources can feel like piecing together a puzzle; without understanding how the pieces connect, you risk ending up with a disorganized mess instead of a coherent image. The key to effective data integration lies in identifying the 'connectors' that align records between datasets.

A reliable connector, or '*key*', is a field that uniquely identifies each record and links it to related information. For example, in employee data, a unique and stable Employee_ID can serve as a key. If you have one dataset with employee performance reviews and another with their training hours, matching Employee_ID across both ensures that the data refers to the same individual.

However, real-world data is rarely perfect. Mismatched or missing keys are common, such as when the same employee is listed under different identifiers or when key fields are absent. Standardizing ID formats, filling in gaps where possible or cross-referencing secondary fields can help address these issues. Detective work, like checking for spelling variations or duplicate entries, can also improve matches.

Choosing stable and unique identifiers is critical. An email address might seem like a convenient key, but it can change over time, unlike an internally assigned Employee_ID that remains constant. Using reliable keys minimizes the need for frequent fixes and updates, keeping your integrated dataset stable and trustworthy.

Consistency in field names is equally important. Small differences, such as one dataset labelling a field 'Dept' and another calling it 'Department' can disrupt the integration process. Establishing consistent naming conventions and creating a data dictionary – a reference document explaining each field – helps maintain clarity and ensures everyone working with the data understands its structure and meaning.

Joining types

Once you've identified the keys and established consistency in your integrated datasets, the next step is determining how you want to combine your data. Joins allow you to merge two datasets based on shared fields, usually a unique ID, so that related information lines up in a single, comprehensive dataset.

When visualized, joins are often represented as overlapping circles, where each circle represents a dataset. The region where circles overlap indicates matched records. Each type of join controls which portions of these circles you end up including in the final dataset.

Figure 8.1   Venn diagram of joins

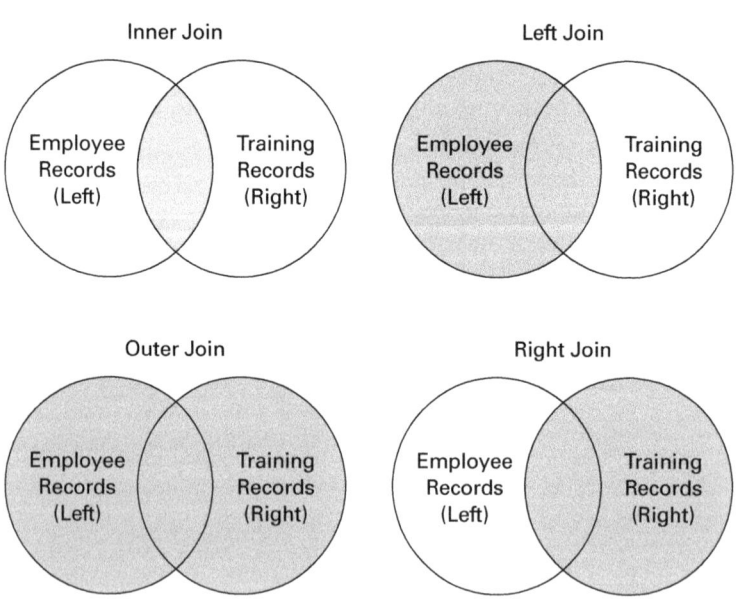

Inner join

An inner join returns only the records that have matches in both datasets. If a particular employee appears in both your main employee dataset and a training dataset, they'll show up after an inner join. If they're missing from one side, they're excluded. Use inner joins when you only need records where both sides have data, perfect for focused, in-depth analysis on fully matched subjects.

Left join and right join

A left join keeps all the records from the 'left' dataset (the one you start with) and adds data from the 'right' dataset where available. If any records in the left dataset don't have a match in the right, they remain, but with empty values (often shown as NULL) for the unmatched fields.

A right join does the same thing in the opposite direction: it keeps all records from the 'right' dataset and tries to match them with the left, filling in NULLs where no match is found. In practice, you'll most often use left joins because you can usually control which dataset you treat as the primary one.

Full outer join (or outer join)

A full outer join includes all records from both datasets, matched or not. If a record isn't found on one side, you'll see NULL values for the missing pieces. This join type provides the broadest view, showing you every record and highlighting mismatches, but it can also lead to a lot of incomplete rows if there are many unmatched entries. Here is some guidance on when to use each type of join:

- **Inner join:** Ideal if you only need rows that exist in both datasets, like analysing relationships that rely on complete information from both sides.

- **Left join:** Useful if you have a main dataset you must preserve entirely, but you'd like to enrich it with whatever related information is available from another source.
- **Right join:** Less common, but handy if your primary dataset is the '*right*' one, or if your tool's interface encourages right joins.
- **Full outer join:** Best for exploratory scenarios where you want to see all possible combinations, spot missing matches or ensure you haven't overlooked any data.

Joining examples

Joining can be a little confusing at first. To illustrate how and when to use each join, let's look at what output we get from each of the join types based on the following datasets:

Table 8.1 Dataset 1 (Employee Records)

Employee ID	Name	Department
001	John Doe	Marketing
002	Jane Roe	Sales
003	Tom Poe	IT
004	Mary Moe	HR

Table 8.2 Dataset 2 (Training Records)

Employee ID	Training Hours
001	10
003	8
005	12

Inner join

An inner join only returns the rows with a match in both datasets. An inner join is useful when you want to focus on records that have information in both datasets, for example, analysing employees who have both an employee record and training data.

Table 8.3   Inner join result

Employee ID	Name	Department	Training Hours
001	John Doe	Marketing	10
003	Tom Poe	IT	8

Only Employee IDs 001 and 003 exist in both datasets, so these are the only ones returned in the newly joined dataset. Employees 002, 004 and 005 are excluded because they don't have corresponding records in both datasets.

Left join

A left join returns all the rows from the left (Employee Records) dataset, and tries to match with the records from the right (Training Records) dataset where available. If there is no match, it returns what is called a 'NULL' for the right-side values. NULL represents missing or unknown data in a dataset. It indicates that no data exists for a particular field, which can impact analysis. Handling these NULL values effectively is important to avoid misleading results.

For instance, if NULL values are found in the 'Training Hours' column, you may decide to exclude those employees from certain analyses or use averages to fill in the gaps – more on this later. Each approach depends on the context of the analysis.

Table 8.4 Left join result

Employee ID	Name	Department	Training Hours
001	John Doe	Marketing	10
002	Jane Roe	Sales	NULL
003	Tom Poe	IT	8
004	Mary Moe	HR	NULL

All the employees from the left (Employee Records) are retained, but for employees 002 and 004, who do not have corresponding training records, the Training Hours column is NULL. Employee 005 is excluded because it doesn't exist in the left (Employee records) dataset.

Right join

A right join works in the opposite direction as the left join. It returns all the rows from the right (Training Records) dataset, and matches from the left (Employee Records) where available. If there is no match, it returns NULL for the left-side values. A right join might be helpful if you're interested in all training records, even if some trainees are not listed in the main employee records; perhaps they are contractors or new hires.

Table 8.5 Right join result

Employee ID	Name	Department	Training Hours
001	John Doe	Marketing	10
003	Tom Poe	IT	8
005	NULL	NULL	12

All employees from the right (Training Records) are retained. However, Employee 005 does not exist in the left (Employee Records) dataset, so NULL values are shown for Name and Department. Employees 002 and 004 from the left (Employee Records) are not included because they don't have corresponding training records.

Outer join

Also known as a full outer join, the outer join returns all rows from both datasets. Where there is no match, NULL values are returned for the missing side.

Table 8.6   Outer join result

Employee ID	Name	Department	Training Hours
001	John Doe	Marketing	10
002	Jane Roe	W	NULL
003	Tom Poe	IT	8
004	Mary Moe	HR	NULL
005	NULL	NULL	12

All employees from both datasets are included. Where an employee exists in one dataset but not the other (like Employees 002 and 004 in the left dataset and Employee 005 in the right dataset), NULL values are shown for the missing fields.

See Figure 8.1 for a visual reference for what is included and excluded for each of the types of joins. Pick the join that best aligns with the goals of your analysis and balance it with the completeness of the dataset it will create. Of note, when joining datasets, especially those containing personal information like employee records, it's important to be mindful of data privacy and compliance regulations. Ensure that you have the proper permissions to access and combine this data.

Data quality considerations during integration

Integrating data isn't just about lining up columns and running a join, it's also about ensuring that the merged result is trustworthy. Before you combine datasets, it's wise to double-check that the formats and data types are consistent. For example, if you're joining by Employee_ID, make sure all IDs are stored as numbers or all as text, and that their formats match in both datasets.

When datasets come together, you may encounter missing matches resulting in NULL values. For instance, if some employees appear in the main record set but not in the training data, you'll see blanks in those training-related columns. Think ahead about how to handle these. Should you exclude them from certain analyses, fill them with a placeholder or investigate why the data is missing?

It's also important to validate that the integrated data makes sense. After joining, pick a few employees or records and manually verify that their details look correct. This spot-checking helps catch any unexpected anomalies introduced by the joining process, such as accidental duplicates or mismatched rows. By paying attention to data quality during integration, you'll save time and build confidence in the analysis that follows.

Enriching data

Data integration is not just about merging what you already have, it's also an opportunity to enhance your datasets. By carefully selecting external datasets that complement your internal information, you can add more depth and context to your analysis. For example, you might bring in industry benchmarks to see how your employee engagement scores measure up against competitors, or incorporate regional economic indicators to understand how market conditions might influence turnover.

In the HR scenario, integrating compensation details, training hours or external labor market trends can transform a simple dataset into a richer resource. Instead of just knowing which employees left, you might see correlations with salary tiers, local unemployment rates or patterns in professional development participation. This richer narrative lets you move beyond isolated metrics, connecting the dots to understand underlying causes and potential interventions.

Common challenges

While working with joined datasets, you'll inevitably encounter common challenges that can complicate your analysis. One frequent issue is duplicates, where joining data produces unexpected redundancies. For example, if one dataset lists employees by department and another details their projects, an employee might appear multiple times after the join, once for each project. Addressing this may require aggregating data to summarize it at the appropriate level or refining your join criteria to ensure each employee appears only once.

Another challenge is varying levels of granularity. One dataset might track monthly engagement scores, while another provides only quarterly results. Directly integrating these can lead to mismatched timelines and confusion. To ensure consistency, you might need to convert quarterly data into a monthly equivalent or adjust monthly data to align with the quarterly format, enabling accurate comparisons.

Staggered update cycles present yet another hurdle. Some datasets refresh daily, while others update weekly, potentially mixing outdated information with fresh data. To avoid this, you can schedule integrations after all sources have been updated or include 'as of' dates in your documentation to clarify the data's currency.

Throughout the integration process, maintaining proper documentation is essential. A data dictionary that defines each field, explains transformations and notes how and when data was integrated can be invaluable. Clear documentation promotes transparency, makes troubleshooting easier and ensures others can understand and replicate your process if needed. By proactively addressing these common issues and keeping thorough records, you'll ensure your joined data is accurate, reliable and ready for analysis.

A note on extraction and integration

As a newcomer to working with data, remember that skilled data professionals typically perform detailed extraction, joining and validation tasks. However, having a high-level understanding of these processes enables you to communicate effectively with data teams and ensures you're clear on what data is needed and why.

With the data extracted, joined and preliminarily validated, you're now ready to proceed to the next stage of analysis, confident that the foundational data is accurate, relevant and ready for further exploration.

Example

Continuing with the HR analytics scenario, your task is to integrate multiple datasets to understand the relationship between training participation, engagement scores and turnover rates for employees in the Software Development department. Previously, you extracted and cleaned the necessary data, and now you'll focus on combining it into a unified dataset that provides a comprehensive view of the situation.

Step 1: Identify common keys

To integrate the datasets, you need a shared field (key) that links them. In this case:

- **HR system data:** Includes Employee_ID, Department and Training_Hours.

- **Engagement survey data:** Includes Employee_ID, Engagement_Score and Survey_Date.

- **Turnover records:** Includes Employee_ID and Turnover_Flag (indicating whether an employee has left the company).

The shared key across all datasets is Employee_ID. Using this key ensures that the data from different systems aligns correctly with each employee.

Step 2: Exclude missing values

After reviewing the engagement survey dataset, you notice that some employees in the Software Development department are missing Engagement_Score values. Rather than replacing these missing values with the department average, you exclude these records from the integration process. This decision ensures the integrity of your analysis by avoiding assumptions about missing data.

Outcome: employees without engagement scores are removed, resulting in a smaller but more reliable dataset for subsequent analysis.

Step 3: Choose the right join

You use a left join approach to integrate the datasets:

1 **Left join 1:** Combine the HR system data with the engagement survey data. This adds each employee's Engagement_Score to the Training_Hours and Department details. Only employees with valid Engagement_Score values are retained.

2 **Left join 2:** Merge the resulting dataset with turnover records. This adds the Turnover_Flag for each employee, indicating whether they left the company.

Step 4: Validate the integrated dataset

After integration, you perform the following checks:

- **Ensure completeness:** Verify that each Employee_ID appears only once in the final dataset.

- **Spot-check records:** Randomly select a few employees and trace their details back to the original datasets to ensure accuracy.

- **Data consistency:** Confirm that numeric fields like Training_ Hours and Engagement_Score fall within expected ranges and that Turnover_Flag values are either 0 or 1.

Step 5: Document the integration process

You document the following:

- Integration steps and any exclusions made (e.g. employees with missing engagement scores).

- A data dictionary, including definitions for fields like Engagement_Score (average score from surveys) and Turnover_Flag (binary indicator of employee status).

Outcome

The final integrated dataset includes:

- Employee_ID: Unique identifier for each employee.

- Department: The employee's department (all Software Development).

- Training_Hours: Total training hours completed in the past year.

- Engagement_Score: Average engagement score for each employee.

- Turnover_Flag: Indicates whether the employee has left the company (1 for yes, 0 for no).

With this dataset, you're now ready to analyse the relationships between training, engagement and turnover. By excluding employees with missing engagement scores, you've ensured that your analysis rests on a solid foundation.

Exercise

For the end-of-chapter exercise, you are given two sample tables that you need to work with. Based on varying objectives, you need to decide which type of join you will need to use to combine the data into a single dataset.

Put on your HR data analyst hat and have a look at the two tables below. Your goals are to get a better understanding of employee engagement, analyse training effectiveness and track supervisor relationships.

Below are the two sample tables. Keep in mind that these are just samples for the purposes of fitting them in the pages of a book; the reality would be that there would be many more rows. However, when working with data, it is typical to work with samples of the data first that are representative of the total dataset without having to wait for the entire dataset to load.

Table 8.7   Exercise employee information

Employee ID	Name	Department	Position	Hire Date
001	John Doe	Sales	Sales Manager	2019-01-15
002	Jane Smith	HR	HR Specialist	2020-03-10
003	Tom Brown	IT	IT Support	2018-07-22
004	Mary Green	Finance	Accountant	2021-05-18
005	Lisa White	Marketing	Marketing Lead	2017-11-02
006	Paul Black	Sales	Sales Associate	2019-10-11
007	Emily Gray	HR	HR Assistant	2022-04-05
008	Sam Blue	IT	Developer	2021-12-15

Table 8.8 Exercise employee training records

Employee ID	Training Programme	Completion Date
001	Leadership Training	2021-02-10
003	IT Security Basics	2019-10-25
004	Accounting Software	2021-06-12
006	Sales Techniques	2020-11-09
008	Advanced Programming	2022-01-20
009	Marketing Strategy	2020-09-17
010	HR Compliance	2021-11-05

Your task is to decide how to join these two datasets so you can identify all employees that have a training record. Basically, you want the employees that are in both tables. What join would you use?

Answer

The join you want here is the inner join. An inner join will return only those employees who have corresponding training records. This is helpful when we need to focus on employees who have undergone training, excluding those without training records. This provides a focused dataset with only trained employees, making it easier to evaluate the effectiveness of training. However, employees without training records are excluded, which might limit understanding of overall training needs so there might be some gaps. See the resulting table below and keep in mind this is based on the sample data above; if more rows were available it would naturally reflect that.

Table 8.9 Exercise inner join

Employee ID	Name	Department	Position	Hire date	Training programme	Completion date
001	John Doe	Sales	Sales Manager	2019-01-15	Leadership Training	2021-02-10
003	Tom Brown	IT	IT Support	2018-07-22	IT Security Basics	2019-10-25
004	Mary Green	Finance	Accountant	2021-05-18	Accounting Software	2021-06-12
006	Paul Black	Sales	Sales Associate	2019-10-11	Sales Techniques	2020-11-09
008	Sam Blue	IT	Developer	2021-12-15	Advanced Programming	2022-01-20

While joining is a technical skill, hopefully you now feel like you understand it enough when you are in conversations with database and IT professionals that you can grasp the foundational benefits and issues that are faced.

Summary points

- **Integration completes the data foundation**
  By combining data from multiple sources, you create a cohesive view that supports more meaningful, context-rich analysis. Integration ensures that all the pieces of your data puzzle fit together before you dive into interpreting insights.

- **A thoughtful approach to joins**
  Selecting the appropriate join type (inner, left, right or full outer) is about balancing inclusiveness with relevance. Understanding the relationships between your datasets and the trade-offs of each join type helps you produce a clean, accurate and useful merged dataset.

- **Data quality and consistency are non-negotiable**
  Smooth integration depends on consistent keys, matching formats and stable identifiers. Addressing mismatches, handling NULL values thoughtfully and validating the final integrated dataset are essential steps to maintaining credibility and trust in the results.

- **Documentation and transparency facilitate long-term success**
  Keeping a data dictionary, documenting integration logic and adopting clear naming conventions not only help you manage complexity in the present but also set up future analysts and decision-makers for efficient, confident work.

Part 5
Analysing data for insights

09

Setting the foundation for analysis

Paving the way

Imagine you're preparing for a road trip. Before you even start the engine, there's a flurry of activity. You plan your route on your favourite mapping tool. You check for road closures, estimate the travel time and look up where you'll stop for petrol or food along the way. You glance at the weather forecast, mentally noting potential rain or snow that might slow you down. Then you inspect your car, tyre pressure, oil level and gas tank, making sure it's in shape for the miles ahead.

At this moment, you're not on the road yet. You haven't reached your destination or overcome any obstacles. But this preparation phase is critical because it ensures you're ready for what lies ahead. Without it, you're at the mercy of unexpected detours, breakdowns or running out of gas in the middle of nowhere.

Similarly, descriptive analysis is the preparation phase for your journey into understanding data. Before you dive into advanced techniques or draw conclusions, you need to get a clear sense of the landscape. Where are the clusters of activity? What patterns are emerging? Are there outliers, like unmarked detours, that could throw your journey off course?

You've spent the earlier chapters of this book assembling your 'vehicle'. You've clarified the questions you're trying to answer, ensured data quality and gathered the right datasets. Now it's time to use that preparation to plot your route. Descriptive analysis is your map, your checklist and your GPS. It provides the foundational understanding you need to guide the rest of your analysis.

In this chapter, we'll introduce you to the tools and techniques for this critical first step. You'll learn how to summarize data with key metrics like averages, variability and distributions. You'll explore how to identify trends, spot anomalies and establish a baseline for deeper exploration. These techniques ensure your analysis is grounded in a solid understanding of the data's structure and behaviour.

By the end of this chapter, you'll have the skills to read the 'roadmap' of your data, navigate around potential hazards and feel confident in the direction you're heading. Because just like any successful road trip, a well-prepared journey into data begins long before you hit the road.

SPOT framework: a path to exploration

Imagine you're standing at the edge of the lake, watching the ripples expand across its surface. To make sense of the signals, you need a systematic approach, one that helps you interpret what you're seeing and guides you to deeper insights. The SPOT framework offers just that: a structured, step-by-step method for transforming raw data into meaningful conclusions.

SPOT, which stands for Summarize, Plot, Observe, Test, provides a structured roadmap for analysing data, starting with a broad understanding and ending with verification of insights. Each step builds on the previous one, ensuring your analysis is thorough, grounded and aligned with your objectives.

The process begins with summarizing your data, where you calculate key statistics like averages, counts and measures of variability. This step provides a high-level overview, helping you grasp the big picture and identify typical patterns or unusual elements. It's like standing on the shore of a lake to understand your surroundings before diving deeper.

Next comes plotting, where you use visualizations to transform raw numbers into clear, interpretable images. Charts and graphs, such as histograms or box plots, make it easier to spot patterns, relationships and outliers. This step is akin to scanning the surface of the lake for ripples that hint at what lies beneath, directing your attention to areas worth exploring further.

Once your data is summarized and visualized, you move on to observing. This step involves carefully analysing the signals revealed through visualizations and statistics, looking for trends, relationships and anomalies that tell a deeper story. It's here that you interpret the meaning behind the patterns, connecting the dots and uncovering insights that may not be immediately obvious.

The final step, testing, validates your findings. It involves questioning initial conclusions, exploring alternative explanations and ensuring that identified patterns are real rather than artefacts of the data or your own biases. This step is necessary for building confidence in your insights and ensuring they are credible and reliable for decision-making.

SPOT complements broader analytical strategies like the BRICE framework, which focuses on defining questions and extracting the right data. While BRICE sets the foundation for preparing your dataset, SPOT guides the process of interpreting it. Together, these frameworks provide a complete pipeline, taking you from identifying what you need to understanding what your data reveals.

In this chapter, we'll focus on the first step: Summarize. Summarizing is the foundation of descriptive analytics, helping you establish a baseline understanding of your data. By calculating central tendencies (mean, median, mode), measures of variability (standard deviation, interquartile range) and identifying outliers, you gain a clearer picture of your dataset's overall structure.

Just like checking your compass before setting off on a journey, summarizing ensures you're heading in the right direction. Once you've established this foundation, you'll be ready to move on to

Figure 9.1   The SPOT framework for analysis

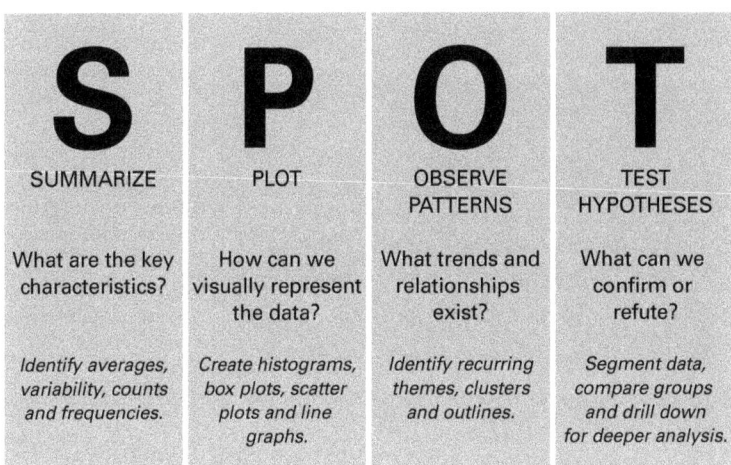

plotting, observing and testing, transforming raw data into action-able insights step by step.

The role of KPIs in analysis

KPIs (Key Performance Indicators) provide the 'why' behind our analysis; they distil organizational goals into measurable targets, as discussed in Chapter 3. While KPIs are invaluable in reinforcing the direction of your analysis, they are not always necessary during exploratory or purely descriptive phases. At this stage, the focus is on understanding the data's structure through foundational meas-ures like averages, variability and distributions. These metrics help you build a comprehensive view of the data landscape, setting the stage for deeper analysis and hypothesis testing.

Even when KPIs are not the central focus, they can serve as valuable guideposts, distilling insights from earlier steps and pro-viding a reference for how trends and patterns might align with organizational objectives. For instance, if your analysis reveals trends that significantly impact a KPI, this can signal areas worth further exploration. However, descriptive analysis often extends beyond KPIs, uncovering unexpected insights that might not directly tie to predefined metrics.

Essential descriptive measures

KPIs provide the 'why' behind our analysis; they keep us focused on the questions and goals that matter most. However, to interpret these KPIs effectively and understand the story they tell, we need a deeper dive into the data itself. This is where descriptive measures come into play. By summarizing the data with tools like averages, variability and distributions, we uncover the context and patterns that make KPIs meaningful. Think of descriptive measures as the lens through which we view and interpret KPIs; they reveal the details behind the numbers, helping us identify what's typical, what stands out and where further investigation is needed. With this foundation, we can confidently move forward in our analysis, grounded in a solid understanding of the data's structure and behaviour.

We'll start by examining measures of central tendency – mean, median and mode – to understand what's 'typical' in your dataset. Then we'll look at measures of variability, like range, variance and standard deviation, to gauge how spread out your data points are from that central point. From there, we'll delve into quartiles and the interquartile range (IQR) to get a finer-grained view of distribution and identify outliers that might merit special attention.

Along the way, we'll distinguish between basic metrics and KPIs. While both provide numerical insights, KPIs have strategic significance, linking directly to your organization's goals. By understanding the purpose and context of each measure, you'll build a versatile toolkit for summarizing data. These foundational statistics not only help you see what's happening beneath the surface but also ensure that, as you progress through Plot, Observe and Test, your interpretations remain aligned with business objectives and focused on driving informed, meaningful decisions.

Average, mean, median and mode

There is plenty of confusion about the term 'average' in the world of data, especially between technical and non-technical people. The reality is, there are several types of average, and each has its own specific use cases and applications. It might seem a little technical, but knowing the types of averages, and when to use them, is an important skill when trying to interpret data. These averages can also be referred to as central tendencies.

Usually, when people talk about 'average' they tend to use the definition of the 'mean' without knowing it. The mean is calculated by adding up all the values in a set and dividing them by the number of values.

Take the numbers 1, 2, 2, 3, 4, 7, 9. There are 7 numbers in this set. So the mean is the sum of the numbers, divided by 7.

The mean is: $(1+2+2+3+4+7+9) / 7 = 28 / 7 = 4$

In this example, the mean is 4.

This gives an overall sense of the trend in the data, but it can be sensitive to outliers or extreme values that can skew the result.

The median is the middle value in the set when it is arranged in ascending or descending order. If there is an uneven number of data points, the median is the middle one. For an even number of items, the median is the mean of the two middle values. The median is useful when dealing with skewed data or outliers as it is less affected by extremely high or low values.

Using our same number set of 1, 2, 2, 3, 4, 7, 9, the median is 3, since that is the middle number in the sequence.

The mode is the value that appears most frequently in a set. It is useful for understanding the most common occurrence in a dataset. It is used mainly for categorical data where we want to find the most frequent category or value. However, it is less commonly used for numerical data.

The mode in this list of numbers 1, 2, 2, 3, 4, 7, 9 is 2 because it is the only number that appears more than once in the set.

Let's now look at how these averages would apply to our HR example and when you should use each one. For this, we will use very simple annual employee salary data. The salaries are in thousands and are as follows:

$$45, 50, 50, 55, 60, 90, 150$$

To calculate the mean, we add all the salaries together and divide by the number of employees, resulting in $500 \div 7 = 71.4K$ dollars. The mean is helpful for understanding overall average salaries and budgeting for salary expenses. However, it can be skewed by outliers, such as the 150K salary in this case, which inflates the average and makes it less representative of typical employee salaries. The mean is most appropriate when the data distribution is relatively even and free of significant outliers. Here, the outlier distorts the overall picture, making the mean less reliable for this analysis.

The median, calculated as the middle value when salaries are ordered from smallest to largest, is 55K. Unlike the mean, the median is not influenced by extreme values, such as the 150K outlier. This makes it a more accurate reflection of a typical employee's salary. The median is particularly useful when outliers are present, as it provides a central value that better represents the data's distribution.

The mode, which is the most frequently occurring value, is 50K in this example. The mode identifies the most common salary paid, which can be useful for understanding trends or salary bands. For instance, HR could use the mode to identify the salary brackets most frequently offered to employees and ensure these salaries are competitive. It is particularly helpful for spotting patterns or dominant categories within a dataset.

In this HR scenario, the 150K outlier makes the median the most useful measure for understanding typical salaries, as it represents what most employees are paid more accurately than the mean. The mode, while insightful for identifying trends, offers a narrower perspective, whereas the median provides a balanced view that is less affected by extremes.

Standard deviation and variance

Averages don't tell the whole story. While they show the central tendency of data, they don't reveal how spread out the values are. Two datasets can have the same average but very different distributions. That's where standard deviation and variance come in; they measure how spread out the data is.

Imagine you're an HR manager tracking employee engagement scores for two teams. Both teams have an average engagement score of 7 out of 10. On the surface, they look the same, but the standard deviation reveals a more detailed picture.

For Team A, the scores are 7, 6, 7, 7 and 8, with a mean of 7. Here, individual scores are close to the average, indicating that employees feel similarly engaged. The small standard deviation reflects this consistency. Team B, however, has scores of 10, 7, 3, 10 and 5, with the same mean of 7. Unlike Team A, these scores are much more spread out – some employees are highly engaged with scores of 10, while others score as low as 3 and 5. This results in a larger standard deviation, highlighting a wider variation in engagement levels.

Despite having the same average, Team A's engagement is consistent, suggesting the HR team's efforts are effective. Team B, on the other hand, has significant disparities in engagement, indicating the need for targeted interventions. The standard deviation captures this variability, showing why averages alone can be misleading. Even the mode for Team B is 10, which could add to the confusion without understanding the spread of the data.

Now that you understand the concept, let's explore how standard deviation is calculated. It's a bit more involved than finding averages, but it offers deeper insights into your data.

First, calculate the mean of the dataset. Then, subtract the mean from each data point to find the deviation, and square each of these deviations to eliminate negative values. Next, find the mean of the squared deviations, which gives you the variance. Finally, take the square root of the variance to calculate the standard deviation.

Let's apply this to Team B's scores of 10, 7, 3, 10 and 5. The mean is 7. Subtracting the mean from each score gives deviations of 3, 0, -4, 3, and -2. Squaring these deviations results in 9, 0, 16, 9 and 4. The variance, or the mean of these squared deviations, is (9+0+16+9+4) / 5 = 7.6. Taking the square root of the variance gives a standard deviation of 2.76. This high value shows that Team B's scores are spread out, reflecting varied engagement levels. In contrast, Team A's standard deviation is just 0.63, highlighting consistent engagement across employees.

As you can see, standard deviation helps uncover hidden details that averages alone cannot reveal. It provides a deeper understanding of your data, helping you identify patterns, variations and areas that require attention.

Quartiles

Quartiles are a powerful tool for understanding and interpreting data, offering insights that go beyond averages or measures like standard deviation. By dividing a dataset into four equal parts, quartiles help us explore the distribution of values, identify patterns and detect outliers. They are particularly useful for analysing large datasets or when a more detailed understanding of data distribution is needed.

To calculate quartiles, a dataset is split into four parts using three key dividing points. The first quartile (Q1) marks the value below which 25 per cent of the data falls, the second quartile (Q2) is the median that divides the dataset in half, and the third quartile (Q3) identifies the value below which 75 per cent of the data lies. Together, these quartiles provide a segmented view of the dataset, helping to answer questions such as whether the data is clustered or spread out, if there are significant differences between groups, or if extreme values might influence the analysis.

One commonly used measure derived from quartiles is the interquartile range (IQR), which is simply the difference between Q3 and Q1. The IQR represents the middle 50 per cent of the data and

Figure 9.2   Quartiles with first and third quartiles plotted

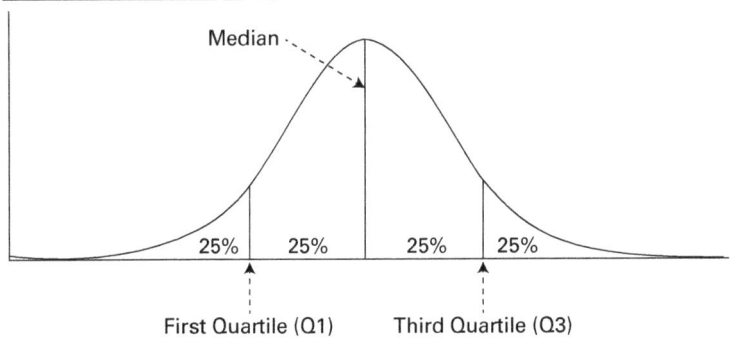

is particularly resistant to outliers, making it an effective way to understand the spread of a dataset. Outliers can often be identified as values falling below Q1 minus 1.5 times the IQR or above Q3 plus 1.5 times the IQR.

Let's apply this to the employee salary dataset: 45, 50, 50, 55, 60, 90, 150.

First, we calculate the quartiles. The median (Q2) is 55, dividing the data in half.

Q1, the median of the lower half (45, 50, 50), is 50.

Q3, the median of the upper half (60, 90, 150), is 90.

The IQR, calculated as Q3 minus Q1, is 90–50 = 40.

These quartiles provide valuable insights: 25 per cent of employees earn less than 50K (Q1), 75 per cent earn less than 90K (Q3) and the middle 50 per cent of salaries fall within a range of 40K.

Using the IQR, we can also identify outliers, such as the 150K salary, which exceeds the upper bound of Q3.

Quartiles are particularly useful in datasets with outliers or skewed distributions, where understanding the spread and identifying key groups is crucial. For example, in employee performance data, quartiles can help HR managers pinpoint the top 25 per cent of performers for promotions or identify the bottom 25 per cent who might need additional training.

Incorporating quartiles into your analysis complements other summary statistics like mean, median and standard deviation, offering a segmented and detailed view of the data. They are also central to visual tools like box plots, which summarize data distribution, central tendency and variability while highlighting outliers. By using quartiles, you gain a deeper and more nuanced understanding of your data, enabling more informed and precise decision-making.

Distributions and outliers

As you move deeper into summarizing your data, it helps to consider how values are arranged, not just their central tendencies or variability. Distributions describe the overall shape of your data, whether values cluster around a centre, are spread evenly or stretch out towards the extremes.

A distribution can be symmetrical, like a mirror image centred around the mean, or skewed, where values bunch up on one side and tail off on the other. For example, employee salaries often form a right-skewed distribution, with most salaries grouped on the lower end and a few much higher salaries stretching out the curve. Recognizing skewness helps you choose appropriate measures of central tendency and understand whether the mean or median is more representative.

Outliers are unusual or unexpected values that are far outside the normal and expected range of your data. Think of them as oddballs, data points that just don't seem to fit in with the rest of the group. As we saw in the averages section, outliers can have a big impact on the conclusions we draw from our data.

Outliers might represent an error in data collection, or an indication of something very significant that needs further investigation. Sometimes, outliers are expected. But, at a minimum, we should understand why they exist and, ideally, how to handle them. Before getting too analytical about the outlier, we should consider the following:

- Investigate the cause: Was there a data collection error, is the data accurate or is there some other data quality issue?

- Remove the outlier: If the outlier is an error, or for some other reason should not be included, remove it from the dataset.

- Analyse separately: Sometimes it is useful to analyse the outlier separately, as it might provide some unique insights that get abstracted when looked at with the wider group.

In our example of employee engagement, an employee with a score of 3 would be considered an outlier when the mean score is 7. In this case the outlier helps us to focus on the employee who would most benefit from some support.

Outliers play a crucial role in detecting unusual behaviour or fraud. In financial transactions, for example, an outlier could indicate unusual activity like an abnormally large purchase made in an unexpected location. Identifying such outliers allows organizations to quickly take action.

Context is important when interpreting distributions and outliers. Are the unusual values a result of data entry mistakes, or do they reflect real-world anomalies, like a sudden surge in overtime hours due to a major project deadline? Understanding the business environment, historical trends and industry norms helps you decide whether to treat outliers as errors to be corrected or essential signals guiding your next steps in analysis.

Avoiding confirmation bias and analytical traps

Even with careful attention to data distributions, outliers and correlations, psychological pitfalls like confirmation bias can still influence your judgment. Confirmation bias, for instance, is the tendency to interpret data in ways that align with your pre-existing beliefs. For example, if you assume high employee turnover is solely due to low engagement and focus only on engagement metrics, you might overlook other critical factors like management practices or compensation issues.

To counteract these biases, it's essential to remain objective and let the data guide your conclusions rather than forcing it to fit a predetermined narrative. Collaborating with colleagues from diverse departments or backgrounds can also provide fresh perspectives, helping to identify blind spots and challenge assumptions. Actively looking for contradictory evidence is another effective strategy – it ensures you're not cherry-picking data to support your initial conclusions. Additionally, validating insights through multiple metrics or KPIs helps confirm the robustness of your analysis, ensuring your conclusions are well supported.

By recognizing these potential analytical traps and taking steps to maintain objectivity, you uphold the integrity of your analysis. Just as a skilled observer interprets ripples on a lake without letting personal expectations cloud their judgment, you too should remain open-minded, flexible and firmly rooted in the evidence before you. This approach ensures your analysis is both accurate and credible.

Example

Returning to the HR analytics scenario, your task is to perform a descriptive analysis on the Software Development team to better understand the relationship between training hours, engagement scores and turnover rates. This team has already been identified as having higher-than-average turnover, including a concerning Q2 spike in turnover rates. Your goal is to uncover actionable insights that will guide the next steps.

Step 1: Summarizing the data

Using the SPOT framework, you focus on summarizing the integrated dataset from Chapter 8. Here's what you find:

1   **Training hours and turnover**

o   Employees who left the team completed fewer training hours on average (mean: 12 hours) compared to those who stayed (mean: 22 hours).

o   Turnover in the Software Development team spiked in Q2, rising from 10 per cent in Q1 to 18 per cent. This aligns with a period of reduced training opportunities following a departmental reorganization.

o   These findings reinforce the hypothesis that limited training participation may contribute to dissatisfaction and turnover.

2   **Engagement scores**

o   The average engagement score across the Software Development team is 7.8, suggesting generally high engagement.

o   However, employees who left the team had an average engagement score of 5.4, significantly lower than the 8.2 average for employees who stayed.

o   Excluding employees with missing engagement scores ensures these results accurately reflect the population.

3   **Outliers and subgroup patterns**

o   A few employees stand out as outliers, with **Training_ Hours** below 10 and **Engagement_Score** below 6. These employees likely represent specific challenges, such as unclear career pathways or lack of support.

Step 2: Observing patterns

The data reveals important patterns that guide your next steps:

1   **Training matters**
There's a clear relationship between training participation and retention. Employees with fewer training hours are more likely to leave. The Q2 spike in turnover coincides with reduced access to training resources.

2 **Engagement as a predictor**
   Lower engagement scores strongly correlate with higher
   turnover, making engagement a key area for intervention.

3 **Financial impact**
   The Software Development team's 18 per cent Q2 turnover
   represents a **$150K increase** in recruitment and onboarding
   costs, contributing to an annualized $500K expense.

4 **Segmenting insights**
   Outliers highlight the need to segment the team into subgroups,
   such as junior versus senior employees or newly hired versus
   tenured employees.

Step 3: Plan for further exploration

Building on these insights, you outline the next steps:

1 **Segment the team**
   o Divide employees into subgroups based on tenure, seniority
     and role type to identify specific challenges faced by each
     group.
   o For example, analyse whether junior developers experience
     lower engagement and fewer training opportunities
     compared to senior developers.

2 **Visualize relationships**
   o Use scatterplots to examine the relationship between
     Training_Hours and **Engagement_Score** for employees
     who stayed versus those who left.
   o Create boxplots to highlight variability in **Engagement_
     Score** across subgroups.

3 **Investigate outliers**
   o Focus on employees with the lowest training hours and
     engagement scores. Review their exit interview feedback
     to uncover underlying issues, such as inadequate
     onboarding or unclear expectations.

Outcome

This descriptive analysis confirms key trends in the Software Development department:

- Employees with fewer training hours and lower engagement scores are at higher risk of leaving.
- Segmenting the team will help uncover subgroup-specific challenges and guide targeted interventions.
- Employees with engagement scores below 6 contribute disproportionately to turnover costs, emphasizing the need for interventions targeting disengaged individuals.
- The financial burden of Q2 turnover highlights the urgency for action.

By explicitly including quarterly turnover rates and financial implications, you strengthen the case for intervention. The next steps in the SPOT framework – Plot, Observe and Test – will build on these insights to create a visual and statistical foundation for decision-making.

Exercise

Imagine you are analysing a dataset of employee engagement scores and years of tenure at your company. Here's the dataset:

Table 9.1   Chapter 9 exercise sample data

Employee ID	Engagement score	Years of tenure
E001	88	2
E002	92	5
E003	70	1
E004	85	3
E005	60	10
E006	95	7
E007	78	4
E008	81	6

1 **Calculate summary statistics**

   o Compute the **mean**, **median** and **mode** of the engagement scores. Which measure seems most representative of the group, and why?

2 **Measure variability**

   o Calculate the **standard deviation** and **interquartile range (IQR)** for the engagement scores. Does the data suggest a consistent level of engagement across employees, or is there significant variability?

3 **Identify outliers**

   o Use the IQR method to identify any outliers in the engagement scores. Are there employees with unusually high or low engagement?

4 **Contextual insights**

   o Reflect on the possible reasons behind the outliers you found. For example, could long tenure (e.g. Employee E005) or short tenure (e.g. Employee E003) correlate with the lower engagement scores? What might this suggest about employee engagement over time?

Summary points

- **Descriptive analysis forms the foundation**
  Before diving into why patterns exist or predicting future outcomes, start by summarizing data with basic measures. This ensures your later insights rest on solid ground.

- **SPOT framework begins with 'S' for Summarize**
  Calculating averages, measures of spread and quartiles provides an initial map of your data's landscape, helping you determine where to focus next.

- **Central tendency and variability matter**
  Mean, median and mode offer different lenses on 'typical' values, while standard deviation and IQR reveal how tightly clustered or widely dispersed data points are.

- **Distributions, outliers and context guide interpretation**
  Recognizing skewed distributions, identifying outliers and understanding the business environment helps you distinguish between anomalies worth investigating and those that can be safely ignored.

- **Beware of biases and traps**
  Confirmation bias and other analytical pitfalls can mislead even the most skilled analyst. Seek multiple viewpoints, consider conflicting evidence and validate your findings with more than one metric.

10
Discovering patterns and trends

Seeing the forest for the trees

Data analysis is like piecing together a puzzle, and the SPOT framework provides a systematic approach to uncover insights from data. Each step in SPOT – Summarize, Plot, Observe and Test – builds on the last to guide you from raw data to actionable decisions. In this chapter we will explore the Plot and Observe steps.

After summarizing the data in the first stage, Plotting (P) is where the numbers come alive. It involves creating visual representations that reveal patterns, trends and anomalies, often hidden in rows and columns of data. Visualization transforms abstract data into something visible and tangible, giving you a clearer picture of what's happening beneath the surface.

Once the data is visualized, the next step is to Observe (O) and carefully analyse those patterns and ask the 'why' behind them. Observation bridges the gap between seeing data and understanding it, uncovering the insights that guide decision-making. Together, Plot and Observe form the heart of exploratory analysis, setting the stage for testing hypotheses in later steps.

Plotting and visualization

Visualization provides a structured and intuitive way to explore data, helping us uncover patterns, identify anomalies and highlight areas that align with or deviate from business objectives. At this stage, the focus isn't on creating polished, presentation-ready visuals but on crafting exploratory sketches that reveal the data's underlying structure and relationships. These initial visuals serve as tools for discovery, allowing us to interpret the data more effectively and answer key questions: What patterns emerge? Where are the outliers? How does the data support or challenge our business goals?

By engaging in this visual exploration, we begin to connect the dots between raw data and meaningful insights, setting the foundation for deeper analysis in the next steps of the SPOT framework.

Data visualization is the process of converting raw numbers into graphical representations, making patterns, trends and anomalies easier to identify and interpret. Visualizations are critical in early analysis because they provide a clear picture of the data structure and allow us to spot nuances that might be hidden in rows and columns of numbers.

Exploratory visualization

Exploratory visuals are created during the analysis process and serve primarily as tools for the analyst. They are not designed for polished presentation but for uncovering patterns, anomalies and relationships within the data. The goal of exploratory visualization is discovery, to flexibly investigate the data, identify trends and highlight areas that merit further analysis. Common examples include histograms for understanding distributions, scatter plots for exploring relationships and box plots for spotting outliers. These visuals are often detailed, iterative and functional, prioritizing insight generation over aesthetics.

At this stage, flexibility is essential. Analysts frequently adjust filters, axes and chart types, refining their visuals as they uncover new layers of meaning in the data. Visualizations might appear 'messy' or complex during this process, but their purpose is to guide analysis, not to communicate findings to an audience.

Creating effective exploratory visualizations requires a focus on clarity and functionality rather than visual polish. It's important to tie each visualization back to the business question at hand. For example, if the goal is to understand relationships between variables, a scatter plot is ideal, while histograms are better suited for examining distributions. Simplifying visuals to avoid clutter is equally important; too much detail can obscure the story the data is trying to tell. Using just enough data to answer the immediate question keeps the exploration focused and efficient.

Colour should be used intentionally, highlighting outliers or key trends without overwhelming the viewer. Clear and concise labels, titles and legends are crucial for ensuring that visuals are easy to interpret. Iteration is also a key part of the process. Starting with simple charts, observing what they reveal and refining them allows analysts to dig deeper into specific areas of interest. Remaining open-minded is critical, as some of the most valuable insights often come from unexpected patterns, outliers or trends that challenge initial assumptions.

Each visualization contributes to building a fuller picture of the data, revealing patterns, relationships and anomalies that might otherwise remain hidden. For instance, a scatter plot could uncover a correlation between training hours and engagement levels, or a box plot might highlight unusually low engagement in a particular department. These insights point to actionable next steps, guiding decisions such as investigating low engagement in Marketing or evaluating the impact of training programmes on employee satisfaction.

Understanding the distinction between exploratory and explanatory visualizations is crucial. Exploratory visuals are for discovery and internal analysis, serving the analyst as a tool to navigate the data. In contrast, explanatory visuals are crafted to communicate findings to stakeholders. Recognizing these different purposes ensures the right visual is created for the right context.

Explanatory visualization

Explanatory visuals, on the other hand, are crafted for communication and are typically presented to stakeholders or decision-makers. These visuals are refined and polished, designed to emphasize key takeaways in a clear and concise manner that supports a specific narrative. Their purpose is not exploration but communication, to convey a message, support a recommendation or tell a compelling story with the data.

Explanatory visuals are visually appealing and focused, avoiding unnecessary details that might distract from the message. For example, a bar chart comparing average engagement scores across departments might include annotations to highlight areas needing intervention. Clear titles, labels and design choices ensure that the audience understands the insights at a glance. Unlike exploratory visuals, which prioritize discovery, explanatory visuals prioritize clarity and accessibility.

While exploratory visuals help analysts make sense of the data, explanatory visuals help stakeholders act on it. Understanding the distinction between the two is essential for tailoring visualizations to their purpose. We will delve deeper into explanatory visualization in Chapter 12, where we explore how to effectively convey data-driven insights to diverse audiences.

Useful charts for exploration

Volumes can have been written about data visualization, and this book is not intended to replace those. However, enough information can be imparted to the data newcomer on the most essential considerations for various chart types. In this process stage, we will look at some charts that will help spot patterns in the data.

Important note: these are not necessarily the charts you would want to use to communicate your findings. They are for data exploration and might be too complex to share and communicate what you are seeing, depending on your audience. Later in the book, we will discuss charts that are more suited to communicating your findings to various audiences.

Imagine data as a forest. Without visualization, analysing it is like examining individual trees one by one, struggling to understand the broader landscape. With visualization, however, we gain a bird's-eye view, allowing us to see the contours, clusters, outliers and gaps all at once. This broader perspective not only makes analysis more intuitive but also guides us toward meaningful questions and insights.

Visualization transforms data into an accessible format, enabling us to grasp in moments what might otherwise take significant effort to uncover. While later chapters will delve deeply into data visualization, it's essential to understand its foundational role in analysis. Effective visualization is not just about aesthetics; it's a vital analytical tool that fosters clarity, accessibility and discovery.

By revealing patterns and trends, visualizations highlight recurring themes in the data, such as increases in engagement scores within a specific department over time, prompting further questions about underlying drivers. They also make outliers easy to spot, as anomalies stand out clearly in visuals like box plots or scatter plots. For example, a department with unusually low engagement scores or high turnover becomes immediately apparent and ready for investigation. Furthermore, visualization helps us explore relationships between variables, such as the correlation between training hours and employee engagement, and simplifies complex datasets, turning dense numbers into actionable insights. These visuals often act as a starting point, directing attention to areas worth deeper exploration.

In the early stages of analysis, exploratory visuals are invaluable tools. They provide clarity, uncover nuances that might remain hidden in rows of data and lay the groundwork for more focused and meaningful analysis. Visualization bridges the gap between raw data and actionable insights, making it a cornerstone of effective data interpretation.

Histograms for understanding distributions

A histogram is a type of bar chart that shows the frequency distribution of a single variable. It divides data into 'bins' or intervals, allowing you to see how often each range of values occurs in the dataset. Histograms help us understand how data is spread out. They can reveal whether data is skewed to one side, has multiple peaks or has any unusual gaps or spikes.

Previously, we discussed the difference between measures and dimensions. For a histogram, the 'bins' or bars represent dimensions of the data. Typical examples of a dimension would be region, product category, customer segment, etc. The height of each bar is then the amount or value of what you are measuring, like sales, number of products or the count of customers.

For a dataset of employee ages across the organization, we want to understand the age distribution. A histogram would let us see how many employees fall into each age range, such as 20–30 years old, 30–40 years old, etc. If the histogram shows a peak in the 30–40 range, it suggests a concentration of employees in that age group. This could guide HR in tailoring engagement initiatives to the predominant age group. You might want to focus more of your analysis on this most significant group as it would be the most impactful to the organization.

This type of visualization can help direct where your attention should go. Depending on the situation, there might be some fascinating details to explore, but if that population is not significant, your time might be better spent elsewhere.

Box plots for spotting outliers and variability

A box plot, or box-and-whisker plot, is a powerful visualization tool for summarizing data distribution and identifying outliers. By

Figure 10.1   Example of a histogram

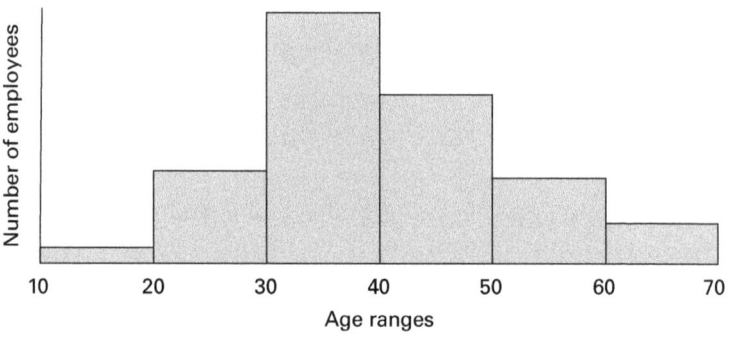

Age distribution across the organization

visually representing the median, quartiles and spread of a dataset, box plots provide insights into patterns, variability and unusual values that might require further investigation.

The box in the plot represents the middle 50 per cent of the data, extending from the first quartile (Q1) to the third quartile (Q3). A line within the box marks the median, indicating the dataset's midpoint. Whiskers stretch to the smallest and largest values within 1.5 times the interquartile range (IQR), while any points beyond this range are displayed as outliers. This structure offers a concise snapshot of key data characteristics: the median reflects the central tendency, the IQR highlights the spread of the middle 50 per cent and outliers point to anomalies or areas that may need further attention.

When applied to employee engagement scores across different departments, box plots provide a clear visual summary of each department's engagement patterns. The median engagement score, represented by the line inside the box, shows the central tendency for each department. The size of the box reveals variability, with smaller boxes indicating consistent engagement scores and larger boxes suggesting more variation among employees. Outliers, shown as points beyond the whiskers, may highlight disengaged or highly engaged individuals who warrant further analysis.

For instance, a department with a wide range of scores and a significant low outlier might indicate uneven morale or engagement challenges. Conversely, a department with a tightly clustered box and no outliers likely reflects a more cohesive and stable engagement pattern. Box plots simplify the complexity of data distribution, making it easier to identify trends and focus on areas that require deeper analysis.

Figure 10.2 Employee engagement box plot

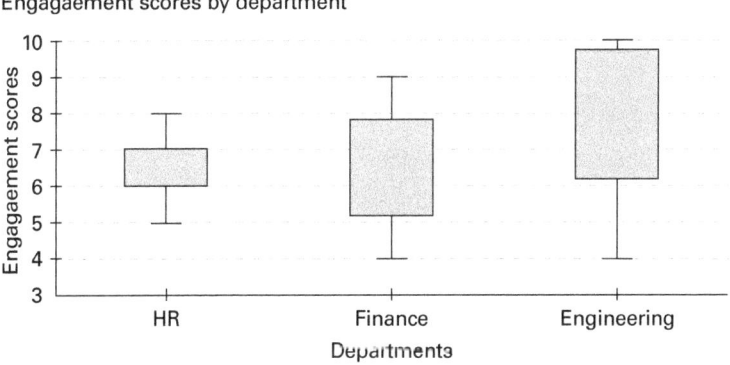

Engagaement scores by department

Box plots help you quickly identify departments or groups requiring attention, compare variability across groups and investigate outliers to understand their root causes or implications.

Scatter plots for identifying relationships

A scatter plot is a simple yet powerful way to visualize the relationship between two numerical variables. Each point on the chart represents an observation, plotted according to its values for two variables, one on the x-axis and the other on the y-axis. This visualization makes it easier to spot patterns, trends or potential correlations that might remain hidden in raw data.

Scatter plots are particularly useful for exploring relationships between variables and can help answer questions such as whether there is a positive or negative correlation, whether clusters or unusual patterns exist or if there are any outliers requiring further investigation. However, it is important to remember that scatter plots show correlation, not causation. Even if a trend appears, it doesn't necessarily mean one variable directly influences the other. Establishing causation requires further analysis, which will be discussed later.

Figure 10.3   Employee engagement versus training hours scatter plot

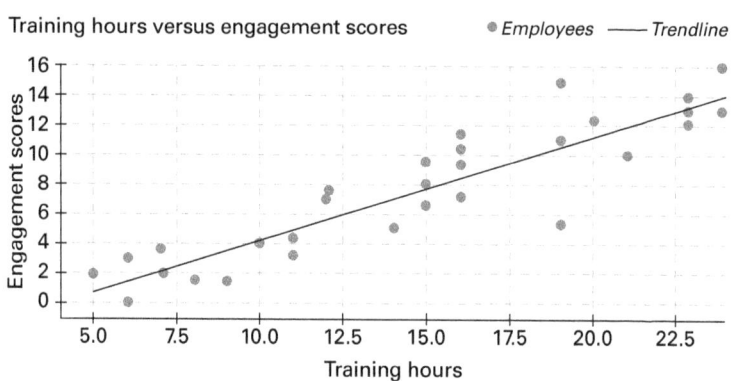

To better understand the relationship between training hours and employee engagement levels, imagine a scatter plot where the x-axis represents training hours and the y-axis represents engagement scores. Each point on the chart corresponds to an individual employee, plotted based on their respective values for these variables. Depending on the distribution of points, the scatter plot might reveal different patterns. A positive trend, where employees with more training have higher engagement scores, suggests a possible positive correlation. If the points appear scattered randomly, this indicates little to no correlation. Outliers, or points that deviate significantly from the overall pattern, might highlight unique cases worth investigating, such as employees who received extensive training but remain disengaged.

Adding a trendline to the scatter plot can provide further clarity. An upward-sloping trendline indicates a positive correlation, while a downward-sloping trendline suggests a negative correlation. A flat trendline points to no correlation between the variables. In the example of training hours and engagement, an upward trendline would suggest that higher training hours are associated with increased engagement. This insight could help HR teams decide whether investing more in training programmes might be an effective strategy to boost employee engagement.

Scatter plots, with or without trendlines, offer a straightforward way to visualize relationships, identify patterns and guide deeper analysis, making them an essential tool in any data analyst's toolkit.

Line graphs for identifying trends over time

A line graph is a versatile tool for visualizing how a variable changes over time, connecting data points with a continuous line to reveal trends, fluctuations and patterns. Typically, the x-axis represents time intervals, such as days, months or quarters, while the y-axis shows the variable being tracked, such as engagement scores, turnover rates or revenue.

Line graphs are particularly effective for time-series analysis, offering insights into trends, seasonality and anomalies. They highlight whether a variable is increasing, decreasing or remaining stable over time, reveal predictable patterns tied to specific periods, such as holidays or quarters, and identify unexpected peaks, dips or changes that may require further investigation. By visualizing data in this way, line graphs provide a clear picture of past performance and can help guide predictions about future trends.

For example, consider a scenario where HR is monitoring monthly employee engagement scores to detect patterns. A line graph could show engagement gradually increasing from January to March, perhaps reflecting the success of a new training programme. It might also reveal consistent dips in June and December, suggesting seasonal factors like mid-year workloads or end-of-year holidays. Additionally, a sudden drop in September could signal an isolated event, such as organizational restructuring or a policy change.

Figure 10.4 Employee engagement scores over time line graph

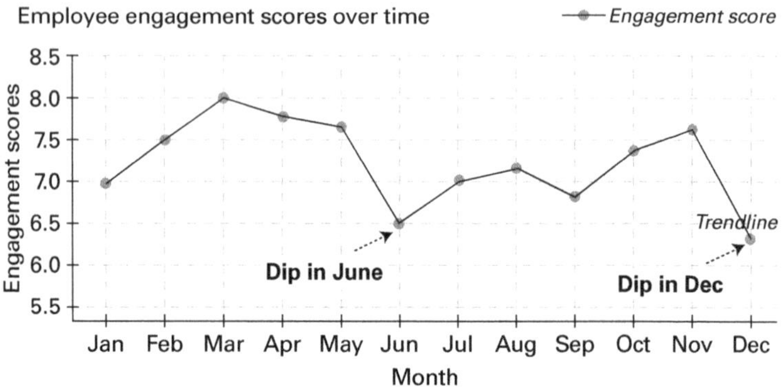

These visual insights are invaluable for decision-making. If engagement dips in December due to holiday distractions, HR could adjust deadlines or introduce morale-boosting initiatives to mitigate the impact. Similarly, an upward trend in engagement following a new initiative provides evidence of its success and supports scaling it to other teams. By tracking changes over time, organizations can proactively address challenges, leverage positive trends and drive continuous improvement. Line graphs thus serve as a powerful tool for understanding and acting on time-related data.

Common pitfalls in exploratory visualization

Exploratory visualization focuses on understanding the data, identifying patterns and uncovering insights during analysis. Unlike explanatory visualization, which communicates findings to stakeholders, exploratory visuals are meant for internal use by analysts. However, there are specific pitfalls that can hinder the effectiveness of exploratory visualization. Here are some of the most common ones to watch for:

Focusing on the wrong question

Exploratory visualization should be guided by a clear purpose or question. Diving into visualizations without a focused objective can lead to wasted effort and missed insights. For example, creating scatter plots to examine relationships between variables without first defining what relationships you're looking for might lead to unclear results. You can avoid this by ensuring you start with a hypothesis or a specific question you're trying to explore from the SMART framework. In addition, you can use visuals to test assumptions or guide further exploration rather than generating visuals aimlessly.

Overloading the visual

Trying to include too much data or too many variables in a single visual can obscure meaningful patterns and make interpretation difficult. A scatter plot that has too many overlapping points or a histogram with an excessive number of bins may make it hard to see any trends. To ensure you don't put too much into the visualization, you can keep it simple by focusing on key variables or limiting the data range. Depending on the tool, you can use techniques like jittering or transparency to manage overlapping points in scatter plots. If needed, adjust bin sizes in histograms to strike a balance between granularity and readability. Remember, a certain amount of complexity is ok for exploration so long as it does not hinder your ability to discern the patterns you are looking for.

Ignoring context

Visuals created during exploration may lack sufficient context, making it difficult to interpret what's being shown or why certain patterns appear. As the person doing the exploration, you may have the context in your head but for others, it might cause issues. A line graph showing monthly sales trends might reveal a dip in a particular month, but without contextual data, such as marketing campaigns or external events, the cause remains unclear. So you might end up reading into something that is really unimportant or has a good rationale for why it exists.

Misinterpreting patterns as insights

In exploratory analysis, not all patterns or correlations in the data are meaningful. Jumping to conclusions based on initial visuals can lead to false assumptions. Similar to the point about context above, care must be taken. To illustrate this point, a scatter plot might show a positive trend between employee engagement and training hours, but further investigation might reveal that a single outlier drives the relationship. For now, treat patterns as hypotheses, not conclusions, until they've been validated through further analysis and the 'T' step of the SPOT framework, where we will test our hypothesis from the progress. If you do encounter some exciting patterns, use multiple visualizations to confirm trends and rule out anomalies or spurious correlations.

Overlooking outliers

Outliers can be valuable for understanding unique conditions or errors, but they're often dismissed during exploratory visualization. Excluding them outright from the analysis can be tempting without properly vetting them. For example, an outlier is ignored in a box plot of department performance because it's considered 'an exception' rather than investigated further. Perhaps the real story is the exception. Instead, highlight outliers in your visuals and examine them separately to determine if they represent errors or insights. Document the reasons for including or excluding outliers in your analysis.

Ignoring variability and uncertainty

Exploratory visuals often focus on central tendencies, such as averages or medians, while overlooking variability and uncertainty, which are crucial for deeper insights. Digging into the variability might provide some hidden gems. A line graph showing average engagement scores over time might mask wide departmental variations. Indeed, averages are sometimes intentionally used for this reason. It's okay to use averages, but you should also complement them with measures of variability, such as standard deviation or interquartile ranges. Box plots are a reliable starting point to show the spread of the data.

Failing to iterate

Exploratory visualization is an iterative process. Stopping after creating one or two charts may lead to incomplete or shallow analysis. It is like peeling back an onion. Sure, you might get lucky, and there are easy-to-find insights laid bare, but usually you will find things that warrant further peeling. You should approach the Plot stage of analysis with the expectation that it might take several iterations to get to the gold. This can include continuously refining the visuals based on emerging questions and patterns. Using combinations of charts and filters will help you explore deeper, especially by exploring the various categories you can slice your data with.

Layering these insights, you create a narrative around the data, one that aligns with your business objectives and drives informed decision-making. This process sets the stage for the next step in the SPOT framework, Observe, where we'll categorize and prioritize these findings to focus on the insights that matter most. For instance, a line graph may show a dip in engagement in Q3. In the next step, we'll explore whether this dip aligns with specific events, such as workload changes or leadership transitions, helping us uncover the story behind the numbers.

Observing patterns

Visualizing data is like climbing a hill to gain a clear view of a forest. Plotting the data gives us that vantage point, transforming raw numbers into visual maps that reveal contours, clusters and outliers. But the journey doesn't end with seeing the forest, it begins when we ask, 'What does this view mean?'

Observing patterns is the step where visuals turn into insights. It's the phase where data starts to tell its story and we transition from creating visuals to interpreting their meaning. Patterns, whether they are trends over time, clusters of similar data points or standout anomalies, are more than just shapes on a graph. They are signals that point to deeper dynamics within a business, audience or process.

The task of observation goes beyond merely identifying patterns; it's about examining their significance. What do these patterns reveal about the underlying data? Are they consistent with expectations or business objectives? Do they highlight opportunities, risks or areas needing further investigation? Each pattern is like a clue, a spike in customer complaints during a product launch, a steady decline in engagement scores within a department or an outlier in sales data, all suggesting causes and implications. The goal is to uncover the stories behind these signals and move closer to actionable insights.

However, interpreting patterns requires caution. Just as not every path in a forest leads to treasure, not every pattern in data holds meaning. Some may be random noise, artefacts of incomplete data or even the result of biases in collection or interpretation. To navigate this, context, critical thinking and domain expertise are essential, ensuring observations are grounded in reality.

In this phase, we'll focus on interpreting trends, clusters and outliers with clarity, exploring how context and domain knowledge refine observations, and discussing common pitfalls in pattern recognition and how to avoid them. By doing so, we move from the raw visuals created in the Plot phase to actionable insights that guide strategy, decision-making and further exploration.

This is where the SPOT framework evolves from seeing to understanding, setting the stage for hypothesis testing and validation in the next chapter. Let's begin the journey from observation to insight, turning what we see into what we know.

Recognizing patterns

Patterns are the fingerprints of your data, distinct shapes and trends that hint at the underlying dynamics of a business, audience or process. Recognizing these patterns is where data begins to speak, offering clues to relationships, behaviours and outcomes that might otherwise go unnoticed. At this stage in the SPOT framework, the goal is to uncover these patterns and interpret their significance in the context of your business questions.

Patterns in data refer to recurring or significant structures, behaviours or relationships that emerge during analysis. They might take the form of consistent upward trends, clusters of similar behaviours or anomalies that stand out from the norm. Identifying and understanding these patterns is a foundational skill in data interpretation and a critical step towards actionable insights.

Temporal trends reveal changes over time, showing steady increases, periodic dips or sudden spikes in the data. For instance, tracking employee engagement scores over a 12-month period might uncover a seasonal dip during the summer months, possibly tied to vacations or work-life balance challenges. Temporal trends can highlight when a problem begins, peaks or resolves, helping organizations anticipate and prepare for future changes.

Spatial patterns uncover differences or similarities based on geographic or locational factors. These might involve comparing regional sales performance, customer satisfaction scores by store location or employee engagement by office. For example, a retailer might observe that urban stores consistently outperform rural ones, prompting deeper investigation into customer demographics or logistical differences.

Clusters are groups of similar data points that naturally form within a dataset, representing customer segments, employee groups or product categories that share common characteristics. Identifying clusters can help organizations tailor their strategies. For example, discovering a cluster of customers who frequently purchase eco-friendly products could inform marketing efforts or inspire the development of new sustainable offerings.

Outliers, the anomalies that deviate significantly from the norm, are another important pattern to examine. While they can sometimes indicate data errors, outliers often highlight critical exceptions. For instance, a department with unusually low employee satisfaction scores compared to others might signal a localized morale issue requiring immediate attention. Outliers can reveal risks or opportunities that might otherwise go unnoticed and often warrant closer examination.

Recognizing these patterns, temporal trends, spatial differences, clusters and outliers is a key step in interpreting data. Each pattern offers a unique perspective, helping to uncover the underlying stories within the data and guiding organizations towards informed decisions and strategic actions.

Understanding trends

Trends reveal the stories data tells over time, showing how things change, shift and evolve. They highlight growth, decline or stability and help businesses anticipate what might happen next. By recognizing and analysing trends, organizations can take a proactive approach, adapting to changes before they become challenges or seizing opportunities ahead of competitors.

Think of trends as the rhythm of your data's heartbeat, offering insights into whether things are running smoothly or signalling potential issues. For those new to data, understanding trends begins with recognizing their forms and approaching them in a structured way. Trend analysis involves examining data over time to uncover changes, patterns and potential correlations. Without this broader perspective, you're left with a snapshot, a single moment in time that might not tell the full story. For instance, a company's sales numbers for December may appear impressive at first glance, but when viewed in the context of previous years, they might simply reflect a recurring seasonal trend rather than exceptional performance.

Looking at data across time allows organizations to gain critical insights. Historical context reveals whether past patterns, such as a dip in engagement scores during the same quarter last year, are repeated. Identifying cycles, like consistent sales spikes every Q4, supports better planning and resource allocation. Analysing trends also helps spot anomalies, such as an unexpected sales drop in Q2, prompting further investigation into underlying causes. Perhaps most importantly, trends form the basis for making predictions, enabling data-driven decisions that shape future strategies.

Recognizing and interpreting trends helps businesses move beyond isolated data points to understand the broader narrative. It's through these stories that organizations can align their actions with the dynamic realities of their environment, ensuring they remain informed, agile and forward-thinking.

Seasonal trends

These are predictable patterns tied to specific times of the year, often driven by external factors like holidays, weather or industry cycles. For instance, retailers may see significant spikes in sales during the holiday season or dips in January as customers recover from holiday spending. Recognizing seasonal trends allows businesses to prepare inventory, adjust staffing or launch targeted marketing campaigns. For example, analysing customer engagement data might reveal a consistent dip during the summer months, likely due to vacations and reduced availability. Knowing this, HR could plan engagement activities or flexible scheduling to counter-act the trend.

Cyclic patterns

Cyclic trends occur over longer, less predictable periods and are often influenced by economic or industry cycles. These patterns might span years rather than months and can signal broader forces at play, such as market demand or consumer behaviour shifts. A tech company might notice a three-year cycle of increased sales every time they launch a major product update. Understanding this cycle allows them to align marketing efforts and product launches accordingly.

Sudden disruptions

Disruptions are abrupt changes that deviate from established trends. They might be caused by internal events, like a policy change, or external factors, such as global economic shifts. While they can signal issues, they also present opportunities to learn and adapt. In our HR scenario, a business might observe a sharp drop in employee engagement scores in Q3. Further analysis reveals that a new performance review system was rolled out during this period. Recognizing this disruption highlights the need to assess and improve how the system is implemented. Of course, having the knowledge that this happened is going to be quite a time saver, rather than having to dig further into a story that might not be there.

Techniques for identifying trends

To effectively identify trends, a structured approach and the right tools are key. Start by plotting data over time using a line graph, one of the simplest and most effective ways to observe trends. Represent time on the x-axis, whether months, quarters or years, and place your variable of interest, such as sales, engagement scores or revenue, on the y-axis. This visualization makes it easier to spot patterns, spikes and dips that stand out.

Using moving averages can further refine your analysis by smoothing out short-term fluctuations and highlighting long-term trends. For instance, a three-month moving average can reveal overarching engagement trends while filtering out month-to-month noise. Comparing data year-over-year is another valuable technique for uncovering consistent patterns like growth, decline or stability, particularly for identifying seasonal or cyclic trends.

Adding context to your visualizations might make some things pop out for you. Annotating major events, such as product launches, policy changes or market disruptions, helps explain the trends you observe and guides future decisions. Always aim to focus on the broader trends that matter rather than getting caught up in minor short-term fluctuations. Pair your observations with real-world events or business knowledge to ensure your insights are meaningful, actionable and defensible. And remember, correlation doesn't imply causation. Exercise caution when interpreting trends, avoiding premature conclusions without further analysis or validation.

Spotting outliers

In many datasets, there are points that refuse to conform, i.e. the outliers. These unexpected, unusual or extreme values stand apart from the general pattern of the data and hold the potential to reveal hidden insights or highlight critical issues. Outliers can signal rare opportunities, anomalies requiring attention or even errors in the data, making them essential to explore and understand.

Identifying outliers is like spotting red flags or golden nuggets in a sea of data. They might arise from human error, unique circumstances or genuinely extraordinary events. However, jumping to conclusions without understanding their context can lead to misinterpretation. Outliers may point to risks, opportunities or errors that need addressing, but focusing on them without proper context can distract from the bigger picture.

Outliers matter in exploratory data analysis because they uncover insights that might otherwise remain hidden. A department with unusually low engagement scores could indicate morale issues or ineffective leadership, while an outlier in customer spending, such as a single customer making significantly higher purchases, might highlight a valuable customer segment worth targeting. Some outliers result from data entry errors or inconsistencies in collection methods, requiring correction before deeper analysis can proceed. Additionally, outliers often spark deeper inquiry, prompting questions like, 'Why is this team underperforming?' or 'What caused a spike in turnover during this month?'

Not all outliers are equally significant, and it's crucial to investigate their cause and context. Determining whether an outlier represents meaningful information or simply noise ensures that your analysis remains accurate and focused. Outliers, when approached thoughtfully, can be key to unlocking the most valuable insights in your data.

Techniques for detecting outliers

Detecting outliers requires systematic methods rather than relying solely on intuition. For those new to working with data, several accessible approaches can help identify outliers effectively.

A good starting point is visual inspection. Charts like scatter plots, box plots and histograms can quickly highlight data points that stand out. For example, a box plot of employee satisfaction scores might reveal a department with significantly lower values compared to others, drawing attention to potential issues.

The Interquartile Range (IQR) method is another approach that we introduced previously. This method focuses on the middle portion of the data. First, find the range of values that covers the middle 50 per cent of the dataset – this is the IQR. Outliers are those values that fall significantly below or above this range. This simple calculation is particularly helpful for identifying unusually high or low values in numerical datasets.

Another approach involves Z-scores, which measure how far a data point is from the average in terms of standard deviations. For example, a very high or very low Z-score indicates that a value is significantly different from the rest of the data. This method works especially well for data that is evenly distributed.

Sometimes, domain-specific knowledge is the best tool for spotting outliers. For example, in a retail setting, any sales transaction over $10,000 might be flagged for review, even if it doesn't stand out statistically. Knowing what is typical for your business can help identify unusual data points that require further investigation.

When working with outliers, it's essential to handle them thoughtfully. They should always prompt investigation rather than immediate action. Not all outliers are errors; some may reflect significant opportunities or rare events. For instance, an unusually high sales figure could represent a major contract win rather than a mistake, highlighting the importance of using business context to interpret outliers.

Outliers can also distort summary statistics like averages. A single department with extremely high turnover, for example, might inflate the overall turnover rate, masking the performance of other departments. By examining each outlier in context, you can decide whether it represents valuable information or should be excluded from the analysis.

Outliers are the unexpected signals in your data. They prompt deeper questions, reveal hidden risks or opportunities and challenge assumptions. When paired with domain expertise, they become a tool for discovery rather than distraction. In the next section, we'll explore how combining data patterns with human knowledge brings clarity to analysis, ensuring even the most unusual data points lead to actionable insights.

Human knowledge and domain expertise

Data can be remarkably revealing, but without the right context, it's easy to misinterpret or overemphasize certain patterns. Observing patterns in data is only half the battle; the other half is understanding whether those patterns are meaningful or just random noise. This is where the human context, domain knowledge, business expertise and situational awareness become critical. Data may provide clues, but people provide understanding.

Patterns can sometimes emerge in data purely by chance, especially in large datasets. It's tempting to draw conclusions from every correlation or trend, but not all patterns are significant. Noise, or random fluctuations in data, can create the illusion of relationships or trends that don't truly exist. The challenge lies in determining whether a pattern reflects a real phenomenon or is just a statistical artifact.

For instance, imagine tracking employee engagement scores across departments. You notice that engagement in one department has steadily declined over the past three quarters. Without further context, it's easy to assume this is a systemic issue within that department. However, if you dig deeper, you might find that the team recently absorbed new hires from a company acquisition, and these employees are still adjusting to the new work environment. The apparent trend could be less about systemic morale issues and more about a temporary adjustment period.

This highlights the importance of applying critical thinking and context to your data analysis. Before jumping to conclusions, ask: What could be causing this pattern? Is there an external factor influencing the data? Could this be random variation? Similarly, in HR, declining employee engagement scores could signify dissatisfaction, but they might also be linked to external factors such as a global crisis or an industry-wide shift. Only someone with a solid understanding of the organizational or industry context can differentiate between internal and external drivers of change.

Domain knowledge also helps analysts ask better questions, such as: What external events might be influencing this trend? Are there organizational changes or policies that could explain the pattern? Does this pattern align with what we know about the business or industry?

Let's consider a practical example of how the human context adds depth to data interpretation. Suppose you're analysing employee engagement scores across an organization and notice a steady decline over the last six months. At first glance, it might appear that overall morale is dropping. However, with some investigation and domain expertise, you uncover that the decline began shortly after a new remote work policy was implemented, requiring employees to return to the office three days a week.

This policy change provides critical context to the observed pattern. The declining engagement scores aren't just a random trend; they're tied to a specific organizational decision. Further investigation might reveal that employees valued the flexibility of remote work and that the new policy has introduced challenges such as longer commutes and disrupted work-life balance. With this understanding, the organization can take action, whether by revisiting the policy, offering additional support or providing clearer communication about the reasons for the change.

Recognizing the human context is an essential step in interpreting data effectively. By combining statistical tools with domain expertise, we can navigate the line between meaningful patterns and noise, ensuring that our conclusions are grounded in reality. This approach not only enhances the quality of insights but also builds trust in data-driven decision-making across an organization.

Clustering

Clustering is a way to uncover groups or segments within data that share similar characteristics, helping you make sense of complex datasets. Think of it as organizing a messy closet: you naturally group similar items – shirts, trousers and shoes – into categories.

Clustering applies this concept to data, revealing natural divisions that might not be obvious at first glance.

In business, clustering helps identify customer segments, group employees by engagement levels or assess product performance in different regions. For example, clustering could reveal three groups of employees: new hires needing more training, mid-career employees with stable engagement and long-tenured staff showing signs of disengagement. These insights allow you to tailor strategies for each group, such as creating onboarding programmes, mentorship initiatives or re-engagement efforts.

At its core, clustering organizes data into groups (or clusters) based on similarities, allowing patterns to emerge naturally. While clustering can be a deep, technical topic often handled by data scientists, here are a few beginner-friendly techniques:

K-means clustering

This method groups data into a set number of clusters by finding similarities among items. For example, in HR, K-means could segment employees based on engagement scores, training hours and tenure. The results might reveal distinct groups like high-engagement new hires or disengaged senior staff. Businesses can use these insights to create targeted strategies, such as improving onboarding for new hires or retention programmes for experienced employees.

Hierarchical clustering

Hierarchical clustering doesn't require you to define the number of groups in advance. Instead, it organizes data into a 'family tree', showing how items group together step by step. For example, a retailer might use it to group products by shared traits like price or category, starting with broader categories (electronics) and refining into subgroups (laptops, smartphones). This flexibility makes it great for exploring relationships when the number of groups isn't clear.

Density-based clustering (DBSCAN)

This technique identifies clusters based on how tightly data points are packed together, treating scattered points as outliers. For example, in analysing customer behaviour, DBSCAN might highlight regular purchase patterns while flagging rare or unusual transactions as anomalies, useful for tasks like fraud detection or identifying rare behaviours.

Clustering simplifies complexity by finding meaningful patterns in your data, even when those patterns aren't immediately apparent. While advanced techniques might require specialized tools, these basic approaches can provide a starting point for exploring trends and making informed decisions.

Bringing observations to life

This chapter has taken us through two pivotal stages in the SPOT framework: Plotting and Observing. These stages mark the transition from raw numbers to meaningful narratives, providing us with the tools to reveal trends, identify clusters and detect anomalies. Together, they represent the bridge between understanding the structure of data and uncovering the stories it holds.

Visualizing data gives us the bird's-eye view we need to see the big picture, whether it's a steady upward trend in sales, an unexpected cluster of customers or an outlier signalling an opportunity or risk. But observing patterns moves us deeper, challenging us to interpret these visuals in the context of our objectives, domain knowledge and critical thinking. Patterns on their own are signals, not answers. They point us towards questions we must ask to uncover the underlying drivers and implications.

By combining visuals with thoughtful observation, we're able to recognize opportunities to capitalize on patterns such as a growing customer segment or an improving metric. We can also mitigate risks by addressing anomalies like a sudden drop in engagement or a spike in complaints. This sets us up for the next step in the SPOT framework: Testing hypotheses.

However, it's important to remember that patterns can be deceptive. They may be the result of noise, incomplete data or unconscious biases. This is why observation must be paired with context and further investigation to ensure our conclusions are grounded in reality. The work done in this chapter is not the end; it's the beginning of deeper exploration. Observing patterns equips us with the insights we need to ask better questions, frame hypotheses and validate or refute our assumptions. In the next chapter, we'll move into the T of SPOT – Testing hypotheses – where we rigorously analyse the patterns we've uncovered, distinguish correlation from causation and transform observations into actionable knowledge.

As you close this chapter, reflect on the visualizations you've created and the patterns you've observed. What do they suggest? What questions do they raise? These reflections are the starting point for the next phase of analysis. Let's carry the insights we've gained into Chapter 11, where we'll test, validate and uncover the truths that drive informed decisions.

Example

You've successfully summarized your dataset, and now it's time to take the next step in the SPOT framework: Plot and Observe. This is where you start transforming raw numbers into visualizations, uncovering patterns, trends and anomalies, and interpreting what they mean within the context of your analysis.

Your refined question is: 'How does training participation affect employee engagement and what patterns can we observe across departments?'

Step 1: Plotting the data

To begin, you create exploratory visuals to bring clarity to the data. These are not presentation-ready charts but tools for investigation, helping you answer critical questions.

1   **Line chart: Turnover trends by quarter**

o   Plot turnover rates for the Software Development team across the past four quarters compared to the company-wide average.

o   Highlight the Q2 spike from 10 per cent to 18 per cent, which exceeds the company average of 9 per cent.

o   **Key observation:** The Q2 spike in turnover aligns with a decrease in training hours and a departmental reorganization, suggesting a compounded effect.

2   **Grouped bar chart: Engagement scores vs. training hours**

o   Compare Engagement_Score for employees with fewer than 6 training hours versus those with 6+ training hours.

o   **Key observation:** Employees with fewer training hours have an average engagement score of 5.4 compared to 8.2 for those with more training.

3   **Scatter plot: Training hours vs. engagement scores**

o   To explore the relationship between training participation and engagement, plot training hours on the x-axis and engagement scores on the y-axis.

o   The scatter plot reveals a positive trend: employees who participate in more training tend to have higher engagement scores.

o   **Key observation:** Training has a measurable impact on engagement, though outliers suggest other factors like onboarding or workload may moderate this relationship.

4   **Bar chart: Financial impact of turnover**

o   Visualize the annualized $500K cost of turnover, with $150K attributed to the Q2 spike alone.

o   **Key observation:** Addressing turnover in Software Development has clear financial benefits, reinforcing the case for intervention.

Step 2: Observing patterns and trends

After plotting the data, you shift focus to the O (Observe) stage, looking for meaningful patterns, clusters and anomalies:

1 **Clusters:** Employees with moderate training hours (6–12) show stable engagement scores, while those with fewer hours (<6) cluster at the low end of engagement.

2 **Trends:** The scatter plot shows a positive upward trend between training hours and engagement scores, reinforcing the hypothesis that training contributes to engagement.

3 **Outliers:** Employees with high training hours but low engagement scores are primarily new hires. This aligns with findings in Chapter 3, where gaps in structured onboarding were identified as challenges.

4 **Seasonality:** The line graph reveals consistent dips in engagement during June and December, aligning with organizational and external factors. These patterns suggest the need for proactive strategies to maintain engagement during predictable downturns.

Outcome

Through the Plot and Observe steps, you've moved beyond raw numbers to uncover actionable insights. Your observations point to:

- a strong relationship between training and engagement, with opportunities to refine training content;

- a financial case for addressing turnover, particularly in Q2, with a potential $150k quarterly saving;

- specific challenges for new hires, reinforcing the need for onboarding initiatives;

- seasonal engagement dips that can be mitigated through tailored strategies;

- to mitigate engagement dips, consider implementing initiatives like mid-year recognition programmes in June or holiday season check-ins in December.

These insights form the foundation for hypothesis testing in the next step of the SPOT framework. You now have clear areas to investigate further, ensuring that your analysis is both focused and impactful.

Exercise

Imagine you are analysing employee engagement scores and training hours in your organization. Here is the dataset.

Table 10.1   Chapter 10 exercise sample data

Employee ID	Engagement score	Training hours
E001	88	12
E002	92	8
E003	70	20
E004	85	15
E005	60	5
E006	95	18
E007	78	10
E008	81	6

- **Visualize the data:** Create a scatter plot to show the relationship between engagement scores and training hours. Label the axes appropriately.

- **Interpret the visuals:** Does the scatter plot reveal a trend (positive, negative or no clear relationship) between training hours and engagement scores?

- **Reflect:** Based on these visualizations, what would be your first step in addressing engagement concerns? For example, would you recommend increasing training hours, or do the outliers warrant further investigation?

Summary points

- **Visualization brings data to life**
  Exploratory visuals like histograms, scatter plots and line graphs reveal patterns, trends and anomalies, transforming raw data into insights.

- **Patterns are starting points**
  Trends, clusters and outliers signal areas for further investigation but require context and critical thinking to uncover their true meaning.

- **Exploratory visuals drive discovery**
  Early-stage visuals are tools for uncovering relationships and guiding analysis – not for polished presentation.

- **Observation turns seeing into understanding**
  Observing patterns involves asking 'why' behind trends and integrating domain knowledge for actionable insights.

- **Avoid common pitfalls**
  Misinterpreting noise, ignoring context or overlooking outliers can lead to flawed conclusions. Pair observation with critical analysis.

- **Insights support decision-making**
  Effective visuals simplify data, guiding both analysts and stakeholders towards informed decisions.

- **Patterns prepare for hypothesis testing**
  The insights from this chapter lay the groundwork for testing hypotheses and validating conclusions in the next step of the SPOT framework.

11
Interpreting results

Proving the point

In the SPOT framework, testing hypotheses is the crucial final step where patterns observed in the data are transformed into validated insights. While summarizing, plotting and observing patterns have given us a clear view of the data's story, this step ensures that the story is grounded in evidence rather than assumptions. Hypothesis testing provides the structure needed to confirm or refute what the data suggests, empowering us to move from informed speculation to confident decision-making.

In Chapter 8, we explored patterns, clusters, trends and outliers, and began to interpret their potential meaning. Now it's time to take a closer look and ask, are these patterns genuine or are they artefacts of chance? For instance, if we observed that departments with fewer training hours tend to have lower engagement scores, how can we determine whether this relationship is real or coincidental? Testing hypotheses allows us to answer these questions with rigour, giving us confidence in the actions we take based on our data.

This chapter will guide you through the fundamentals of hypothesis testing, from crafting clear, testable statements to choosing the right methods and interpreting results. By the end of this chapter, you'll understand how to apply this essential skill to ensure that your data-driven decisions are backed by sound evidence. Hypothesis testing not only validates insights but also refines our understanding of the data, often leading to new questions and deeper analysis. It's the step that turns observation into proof and sets the foundation for strategic, data-driven action.

So let's dive in and explore how to put our observations to the test, ensuring that our decisions rest on a solid foundation of evidence.

What is hypothesis testing?

At its core, hypothesis testing is a structured process for validating patterns in data. It's a method for asking, 'Is what we're observing real, or is it just random noise?' Think of it as a systematic way to evaluate whether a pattern or relationship truly exists and whether it holds up under scrutiny.

Consider this simple analogy: imagine you've started taking a new route to work and you feel like it's getting you there faster. Hypothesis testing is like timing both your old and new routes over several days to see if the new one consistently saves you time or if that impression was just a one-off fluke. It's a way to gather evidence and remove doubt from your decision-making. In data analysis, hypothesis testing works the same way. If we've observed a pattern, like employees with more training hours having higher engagement scores, hypothesis testing helps us determine whether this relationship is significant or simply coincidental. It's a process of going beyond 'This seems true' to 'We've confirmed this with data.'

Hypothesis testing matters because it transforms observation into action. Patterns in data might seem compelling at first glance, but without testing, there's always the risk of making decisions based on false assumptions. Acting on a pattern that doesn't hold up can lead to wasted resources, missed opportunities or unintended consequences. By rigorously testing hypotheses, we gain confidence in our findings. For example, instead of assuming that offering more training improves engagement, we can confirm whether this relationship is real. Or rather than attributing a spike in sales to a marketing campaign, we can test whether the campaign had a measurable impact.

In short, hypothesis testing reduces uncertainty, allowing us to base decisions on evidence rather than guesswork. It helps ensure that our data-driven strategies are grounded in reality, minimizing risk and increasing the likelihood of success. Testing is the final step in the SPOT framework and the culmination of everything we've done so far. After summarizing the data to understand its key characteristics, plotting it to visualize its structure and observing patterns to uncover trends, clusters and outliers, we're now ready to test whether these patterns hold true.

For example, in the last chapter, we identified clusters of employees with low engagement scores and limited training hours. Testing allows us to determine whether a lack of training is a significant factor in low engagement. Similarly, if we observed that marketing campaigns seem to drive higher sales in certain regions, testing helps us confirm whether this effect is statistically significant or merely a coincidence. Hypothesis testing ensures that this process isn't happening in isolation. It's the logical next step in our journey, turning patterns into proof and paving the way for confident, data-driven decisions.

Formulating hypotheses

A hypothesis is a testable statement that explains a relationship or pattern observed in your data. It serves as the foundation of hypothesis testing, providing a clear direction for your analysis and helping determine whether an idea holds true. Essentially, a hypothesis transforms a question into a statement that can be evaluated with evidence.

For instance, if you observe that employees with more training hours tend to have higher engagement scores, you might formulate a hypothesis such as: 'Employees who complete more training hours have higher engagement scores compared to those who complete fewer training hours.' This statement is specific and testable, enabling you to gather data and assess whether the observed pattern is genuine or coincidental.

Not all hypotheses are equally effective. A strong hypothesis is clear, specific and directly tied to observed patterns or critical business questions. It should define the variables being tested and articulate the expected relationship between them. Additionally, it must be testable and measurable, providing a framework for gathering evidence to support or refute it. For example, a well-structured hypothesis might state: 'Departments with higher overtime hours have higher employee turnover rates.' This is both specific and quantifiable. In contrast, a vague hypothesis like 'Overtime is bad' is untestable and lacks the clarity needed for meaningful analysis.

Hypothesis testing relies on two key concepts: the null hypothesis and the alternative hypothesis. The null hypothesis (H_0) assumes no effect or relationship between the variables, serving as the baseline assumption that any observed pattern is due to random chance. For example, the null might state, 'Training hours have no impact on engagement scores.' The alternative hypothesis (H_1), on the other hand, posits that there is a relationship or effect between the variables, such as, 'Training hours increase engagement scores.' The goal of hypothesis testing is to gather evidence to either reject the null hypothesis in favour of the alternative or fail to reject the null, indicating no significant relationship was found.

The null hypothesis is essential because it provides a structured starting point, ensuring that conclusions are based on rigorous testing rather than assumptions. For example, in examining overtime and turnover, the null hypothesis might state, 'Overtime hours have no impact on turnover rates', while the alternative suggests, 'Higher overtime hours are associated with higher turnover rates.' By collecting and analysing data, you aim to determine whether enough evidence exists to reject the null hypothesis and support the alternative.

Formulating clear, measurable and testable hypotheses is crucial for meaningful analysis. A well-defined hypothesis sets the stage for structured inquiry, turning observations into actionable insights. With a hypothesis in hand, the next step is to select the appropriate methods for testing it, ensuring your analysis is both rigorous and insightful.

Techniques for hypotheses testing

Testing hypotheses involves structured methods to analyse data and determine whether the patterns you've observed are meaningful. For those new to data, this doesn't require diving into complex statistical models; there are plenty of accessible techniques to get started. Three effective methods are A/B testing, cross-tabulation and basic statistical tests.

A/B testing

A/B testing is a straightforward way to compare two groups and evaluate whether one performs better than the other. Commonly used in marketing, product development and HR analytics, this method involves creating two groups: a control group (Group A), where no changes are made, and a test group (Group B), where a change is introduced. For example, imagine you're testing whether offering flexible work hours improves employee satisfaction. Group A continues with regular hours, while Group B is given flexible hours. After three months, you survey both groups and analyse their satisfaction scores. If Group B shows significantly higher scores, you have evidence that flexible hours positively impact satisfaction.

Cross-tabulation

Cross-tabulation is another simple and accessible technique, especially for exploring relationships between two categorical variables. It involves creating a table (a 'cross-tab') to display how these variables interact, revealing patterns that might not be immediately obvious. For instance, if you're investigating employee turnover, you could cross-tabulate turnover rates by department. Each row of the table represents a department, while the columns show how many employees stayed versus left. If you notice higher turnover rates in departments like Marketing and Sales, this insight can guide further investigation into challenges such as workload, leadership or development opportunities.

Statistical testing

Statistical testing, such as t-tests and chi-square tests, provides a way to determine whether differences between groups or relationships between variables are statistically significant. A t-test compares the averages of two groups to see if the difference is likely due to a real effect or random chance. For example, if one department participated in a training programme and another did not, a t-test can help determine whether differences in their engagement scores are meaningful. A chi-square test, on the other hand, examines relationships between categorical variables. For instance, you might analyse whether turnover rates differ significantly between employees with short, medium or long tenure. This could help identify groups that might need targeted retention efforts.

For a newcomer, these techniques might sound intimidating, but they don't have to be. Many tools, such as Excel or Power BI (and of course Python and R) make it accessible to conduct these tests without deep technical knowledge. The key is to focus on the business question you're trying to answer and choose the method that best aligns with your data and objectives.

Segmenting and comparing

One of the most effective ways to make hypothesis testing meaningful is by segmenting your data into relevant groups and comparing them. Segmentation divides a dataset into smaller, meaningful groups based on shared characteristics, such as department, tenure or location. This process adds nuance to your analysis, allowing you to identify unique patterns or differences that might be obscured when looking at the data as a whole. By focusing on specific subgroups, segmentation helps ensure your insights are actionable and reduces the risk of making broad generalizations from incomplete information.

For example, while overall employee engagement scores may appear steady, segmenting the data by tenure could reveal that new hires with less than a year of experience consistently score lower than more seasoned employees. Without segmentation, this insight would remain hidden, potentially causing missed opportunities to address key issues.

Segmenting data enables you to pinpoint specific areas for action, focusing your efforts where they're most needed rather than addressing issues organization-wide. It ensures fairness in your analysis by avoiding over-generalizations and considering how variables impact different groups. Furthermore, segmentation allows you to tailor interventions to the needs of specific segments, such as designing targeted engagement programmes for new hires or role-specific training for managers.

Breaking your data into meaningful groups requires thoughtful planning to align the segments with your business questions. Start by identifying relevant categories that might influence the patterns you're analysing. Common segmentation variables include tenure, department, location, demographics (such as age or role level) and behavioural metrics like training hours or performance ratings. For instance, segmenting employees by tenure into groups such as less than one year, one to five years and over five years can help explore how engagement varies across experience levels.

Visualizations can also guide segmentation. Histograms might reveal clusters of employees with different levels of training, while scatter plots of satisfaction scores by location could highlight regional disparities. Once you've identified the segments, structure your data to enable easy comparisons. For example, compare sales performance between urban and rural locations to uncover geographic differences or group employees by tenure to identify specific engagement challenges.

It's also important to ensure balanced group sizes whenever possible. If one group is disproportionately smaller than others, it could skew your results and introduce bias into your analysis. Thoughtful segmentation not only enhances the depth of your analysis but also ensures your findings are both accurate and actionable, providing a strong foundation for targeted decision-making.

Hypothesis results

Testing a hypothesis is not just about numbers; it's about turning those numbers into insights that guide action. Interpreting results effectively ensures that the conclusions drawn are meaningful and aligned with your goals. Statistical significance is a way to determine whether the results of your test are likely due to the pattern you've observed or simply due to random chance. In simple terms, it's like asking, 'Is this result real, or did it just happen by accident?'

Imagine flipping a coin. If you flip it five times and it lands on heads every time, you might start to wonder if the coin is biased. However, this outcome could also happen by chance, even if the coin is fair. Statistical significance helps us quantify the likelihood of this result happening randomly. If the probability is very low (usually less than 5 per cent, or a p-value <0.05), we conclude that the result is significant and likely not random.

In the context of data analysis, statistical significance helps you confirm whether patterns, like the impact of training hours on engagement scores, are genuine or simply coincidences. It adds a layer of confidence to your decisions, ensuring that you're acting on reliable insights.

While statistical tests provide valuable insights, they come with limitations and potential pitfalls. A p-value indicates the probability of your result occurring by chance, but it doesn't tell the whole story. For example, a statistically significant result might not always be practically significant. In other words, just because a pattern is real doesn't mean it's important or actionable. Always consider the magnitude of the effect and its relevance to your goals.

For example, if a test reveals that a training programme improves engagement scores by 0.1 per cent, this might be statistically significant but not impactful enough to justify the cost of the program.

Correlation and causation

Are ice cream sales correlated with shark attacks? During the summer months, both ice cream sales and shark attacks tend to increase. This might lead someone to believe that consuming ice cream somehow causes shark attacks. However, this is a clear case of correlation without causation. The real cause of both increases is the hot weather. As temperatures rise, more people go to the beach, increasing both ice cream consumption and shark attacks, as more people are in the water. While it is a simple example, it illustrates why we need to be careful when two variables that seem correlated may not have a cause-and-effect relationship.

Correlation is a statistical relationship between two or more variables. When variables are correlated, it means changes in one variable are associated with changes in the other. However, it does not imply that one variable is causing the other to change. There are several types of correlation. Positive correlation occurs when one variable increases, the other increases (e.g. height and weight). Negative correlation is when one variable increases, the other decreases (e.g. hours spent studying and incorrect answers in a test). No correlation occurs when there is no consistent pattern between the variables (e.g. shoe size and job satisfaction).

In statistics, correlation is expressed as a correlation coefficient, a number between -1 and $+1$. The closer the coefficient is to $+1$ or -1, the stronger the relationship.

Causation means that one variable directly causes a change in another. Establishing causation is more complex than correlation and will often involve deeper statistical analysis. People often confuse correlation with causation, leading to incorrect conclusions.

We must be very deliberate when making the leap from correlation to causation. Correlation highlights relationships between variables, while causation demonstrates direct influence. Jumping to conclusions by assuming causation from a correlation is a fast way to lose trust and credibility.

To further illustrate the care that must be taken, let's look at an example for our HR scenario. After looking at the data, you observe a positive correlation between the number of sick days an employee takes and their likelihood of leaving the company. It looks like the correlation is a strong one, suggesting that an employee who takes more sick days is more likely to resign. However, and this is where we need to be careful, this does not automatically mean that taking sick days causes employees to leave.

In order to prove causation, you would need to probe in more detail. Perhaps, after analysis, you find that poor supervisor relationships are causing both more sick days (due to stress and burnout) and higher turnover rates. In this case, you have established causation: poor supervisor relationships are the underlying cause of both increased sick days and employee resignations.

Common pitfalls

Hypothesis testing is a powerful tool for validating patterns and making data-driven decisions. However, it's also easy to misstep along the way. To ensure your analysis is both accurate and meaningful, it's essential to recognize and avoid some common pitfalls. These challenges can undermine the validity of your findings and lead to misguided conclusions.

Bias and preconceived notions

One of the most common pitfalls in hypothesis testing is allowing bias or preconceived notions to influence the process. When you approach data with a strong expectation or agenda, there's a risk of designing tests or interpreting results in a way that confirms what you already believe, rather than uncovering the truth.

For example, imagine you believe that employees with more training hours are always more engaged. If you only test data from departments where training is known to be highly effective, you may overlook cases where training had little to no impact. This selective approach can skew your results and reinforce incorrect assumptions.

Start with an open mind and let the data guide your conclusions. Use neutral language in your hypothesis, and ensure your data sample represents a broad, unbiased view of the issue you're investigating.

Small sample sizes

Drawing conclusions from a small or unrepresentative sample can lead to unreliable results. Small samples increase the likelihood of random variation affecting your outcomes, making it harder to detect meaningful patterns or relationships. For instance, if you're analysing turnover rates in a department with only five employees, one resignation could dramatically skew your findings. While this might indicate an issue in that specific team, it doesn't provide enough evidence to generalize about turnover across the organization. Whenever possible, ensure your sample size is large enough to provide statistical power. This means having enough data points to detect real effects while minimizing the influence of random noise. If your dataset is small, acknowledge this limitation and treat your conclusions as preliminary.

Ignoring context

Data doesn't exist in a vacuum, and neither should your analysis. Hypothesis testing without considering the broader context can lead to misinterpretations or oversights. For example, a spike in customer complaints might seem like a service issue at first glance, but a closer look might reveal it coincided with a major product recall. Context also matters when interpreting statistical results. A small but statistically significant change might have limited practical impact, while a non-significant result might still hold value when paired with qualitative insights or domain expertise. Always incorporate domain knowledge into your analysis. Collaborate with subject matter experts to interpret results in light of business realities, and consider external factors that might influence the data.

Misinterpreting results

Statistical significance is often misunderstood or misused. A significant result doesn't necessarily mean the effect is large or important, and a non-significant result doesn't always mean there's no effect. Similarly, generalizing findings too broadly can lead to poor decision-making. For example, if a test shows that training improves engagement in one department, it doesn't mean the same strategy will work across all teams. Factors like team dynamics, leadership and workload may vary widely, influencing the outcome. When interpreting results you need to distinguish between statistical and practical significance. Ask yourself, 'Is this effect meaningful in the real world?' Avoid overgeneralizing findings and try to limit your conclusions to the specific context of your analysis unless further testing supports broader applications.

By recognizing these common pitfalls and taking steps to mitigate them, you can ensure your hypothesis testing is both robust and actionable. The key is to approach the process with curiosity, care and a commitment to evidence over assumptions. This will help you draw insights that truly align with your data and organizational goals.

From hypothesis to insight

Hypothesis testing is the final step in the SPOT framework, transforming patterns and observations into validated insights. It's where we move beyond assumptions and into the realm of evidence-based decision-making. By systematically testing our hypotheses, we ensure that the conclusions we draw are rooted in data, not guesswork. This step isn't just about confirming or rejecting ideas, it's about deepening our understanding. Each hypothesis we test adds another layer to the story our data is telling, helping us uncover the 'why' behind the patterns we observe. Whether it's identifying the root causes of employee disengagement or pinpointing the impact of a new marketing campaign, hypothesis testing bridges the gap between exploration and action.

Yet, this is not the end of the journey. Hypothesis testing often raises new questions and reveals deeper insights, creating a natural cycle within the SPOT framework. Each validated (or invalidated) hypothesis leads to new data to summarize, patterns to observe and further questions to test. This iterative process allows us to refine our understanding and continue improving our strategies.

Now, with tested hypotheses in hand, we're ready for the final, and arguably the most difficult, stages: turning insights into action. In Chapter 12, we'll explore how to effectively communicate these insights to stakeholders, ensuring they drive meaningful decisions and strategies. We'll discuss the power of data visualization and storytelling in making complex ideas clear, compelling and actionable.

Example

In the last chapter, you observed a concerning trend: the Software Development team consistently had lower engagement scores and fewer training hours compared to other departments. A scatter plot suggested a positive correlation between training hours and engagement scores, but you know it's essential to validate this observation through hypothesis testing. Is the lack of training truly impacting engagement, or is this pattern coincidental?

Your hypothesis is straightforward: 'Employees in the Software Development team with more training hours have higher engagement scores.'

Step 1: Formulating hypotheses

You structure your analysis by defining the null and alternative hypotheses:

- **Null hypothesis (H_0):** Training hours have no impact on engagement scores within the Software Development team.

- **Alternative hypothesis (H_1):** Training hours positively influence engagement scores within the Software Development team.

By framing the null hypothesis, you ensure an objective starting point for your test, making it clear that you're looking for evidence to reject it in favour of the alternative.

Step 2: Testing the hypothesis

To test your hypothesis, you segment the Software Development team into two groups: employees with fewer than 10 training hours (low training group) and those with 10 or more training hours (high training group). You then compare their average engagement scores.

1 **A/B testing**

    Using an A/B test, you calculate the average engagement scores for both groups within Software Development:

    o **Low training group:** Average engagement score = **5.4**

    o **High training group:** Average engagement score = **8.2**

A t-test reveals a **p-value of 0.02**, which is below the standard threshold of 0.05. This indicates that the observed difference in engagement scores is statistically significant and unlikely due to random chance.

    Result: You reject the null hypothesis, confirming that higher training hours are associated with higher engagement scores in the Software Development team.

1 **Cross-tabulation with other departments**
   To ensure this pattern is unique to Software Development, you compare it with other departments using cross-tabulation:

   o Other teams also show a positive relationship between training and engagement, but the effect is most pronounced in Software Development. This aligns with descriptive statistics from Chapter 9, where Software Development had the lowest average engagement scores among teams.

2 **Identifying outliers**
   Revisiting the scatter plot from Chapter 10, you notice a few Software Development employees with high training hours but low engagement scores. By segmenting these employees by tenure, you discover that they are primarily **new hires**.

   This finding ties back to Chapter 3, where a lack of structured onboarding was identified as a challenge. It suggests that while training is beneficial, new hires may need additional support, such as onboarding or mentoring, to fully engage.

Step 3: Interpreting results

Your findings confirm that training hours significantly impact engagement within the Software Development team. However, the analysis also uncovers nuances:

1 **Department-specific impact:** The relationship between training and engagement is strongest in Software Development, emphasizing the need for targeted interventions.

2 **Support for new hires:** Training alone does not address engagement challenges for new hires, pointing to a need for enhanced onboarding and mentorship programmes.

3 **Financial implications:** Addressing training-related engagement challenges could save the company an estimated $150K per quarter, reducing the annualized $500K turnover expense.

These results are consistent with earlier findings:

- Chapter 9 highlighted that employees with fewer training hours had lower engagement scores (**5.4 for leavers vs. 8.2 for stayers**).
- Chapter 3 identified gaps in onboarding and career development as drivers of disengagement, further supported by outlier analysis here.

Step 4: Avoiding pitfalls

Throughout the process, you ensure:

- **Sufficient sample size:** The Software Development team sample is large enough to yield reliable results.
- **Contextual interpretation:** High turnover rates and workload pressures, discussed in earlier chapters, are factored into your analysis.
- **Causal caution:** While the findings indicate a strong relationship between training and engagement, you avoid assuming causation without further investigation.

Step 5: Next steps

Based on these results, you prepare actionable recommendations for leadership:

1 **Invest in tailored training programmes:** Develop training specifically designed for the needs of Software Development employees, aligned with insights from Chapter 9.

2 **Enhance onboarding and mentorship:** Address challenges for new hires, reinforcing the need for onboarding programmes identified in Chapter 3.

3 **Monitor engagement over time:** Use regular engagement surveys to track progress and refine interventions, as suggested in Chapter 10.

Closing the loop

Testing your hypothesis has turned an observed pattern into a validated insight, allowing you to recommend evidence-based actions. However, the findings also raise new questions:

- Why does training have such a pronounced impact in Software Development compared to other teams?

- Are additional factors, like leadership or workload, influencing engagement scores?

These questions will guide the next iteration of your analysis. When presenting these findings, use visuals such as scatterplots and bar charts from Chapter 10 to clearly illustrate the relationship between training hours and engagement scores. Highlight financial implications to build a compelling case for leadership intervention.

With validated insights, you've completed the SPOT framework and are ready to move on to effectively communicating findings to stakeholders. In the next chapter, you'll learn how to craft compelling visualizations and narratives to ensure your insights lead to meaningful action.

Exercise

Using the same dataset from Chapter 10, evaluate whether training hours have a significant effect on employee engagement.

1 **Formulate a hypothesis**

- Null Hypothesis (H_0): Training hours have no impact on engagement scores.

- Alternative Hypothesis (H_1): Training hours have a positive impact on engagement scores.

2 **Analyse the data**

- o Calculate the correlation coefficient between training hours and engagement scores.

- o Split the dataset into two groups:

  - – Group 1: Employees with 10 or fewer training hours.

  - – Group 2: Employees with more than 10 training hours.

- o Compare the mean engagement scores of the two groups.

3 **Interpret results**

- o Is there a meaningful correlation between training hours and engagement scores? What does the comparison between the two groups suggest?

- o Based on your analysis, what recommendations would you make to improve engagement in the organization?

Summary points

- • **Hypothesis testing validates observations**
  Hypothesis testing ensures patterns and trends observed in data are grounded in evidence, turning speculation into confidence for decision-making.

- • **Clear hypotheses are crucial**
  A good hypothesis is specific, measurable and testable. Use both null and alternative hypotheses to structure testing and maintain objectivity.

- • **Techniques to test hypotheses**
  Use accessible methods like A/B testing, cross-tabulation and basic statistical tests (e.g. t-tests, chi-square) to evaluate patterns and relationships in data.

- • **Segment data for deeper insights**
  Breaking data into meaningful groups, such as by department or tenure, reveals nuanced patterns and helps target interventions more effectively.

- **Statistical significance vs. practical relevance**
  Significant results indicate patterns are unlikely due to chance, but always evaluate their real-world impact before making decisions.

- **Beware of common pitfalls**
  Avoid bias, small sample sizes, ignoring context and confusing correlation with causation. Use domain knowledge to guide interpretations.

- **From testing to actionable insights**
  Hypothesis testing refines understanding, validates data-driven decisions and often reveals new questions to explore, creating a cycle of continuous improvement.

Part 6
Communicating insights and driving decisions

12
Influencing decisions

Making an impact

Imagine spending weeks wrangling a dataset, meticulously cleaning, analysing and interpreting every detail. You uncover compelling insights that could improve efficiency or significantly reduce costs, but somehow those insights never translate into real-world decisions. The stumbling block often isn't the quality of the data or analysis, it's the way the story is told. Like in previous chapters, following a framework can help simplify the approach.

ACTED, which stands for Audience, Context, Tale, Envision and Delivery, bridges the gap between raw data insights and actionable decisions through structured storytelling. It addresses common pitfalls in communicating data-driven findings, ensuring your narrative engages the audience, clarifies the 'why' behind the numbers and provides a clear path to action. Each stage of the framework is designed to overcome barriers that frequently derail efforts to turn insights into initiatives.

Many organizations, despite aspiring to build 'data-driven cultures' struggle to get stakeholders on board. Presentations often fail because the messaging is misaligned with the audience. Technical details might overwhelm executives focused on strategy, while overly simplistic overviews leave technical teams feeling unsatisfied. Irrelevant or poorly designed visuals can obscure key points, focusing on the wrong metrics or creating confusion. Insights themselves can feel disconnected, highlighting a problem without explaining why it matters or offering solutions. Even when stakeholders understand the insight, they may feel uncertain about the next steps or lack the empowerment to implement changes.

The ACTED framework addresses these challenges by helping you craft data stories that resonate with diverse audiences, align with organizational goals and inspire action. In this chapter, we'll explore each step of ACTED, showing how to transform raw data into compelling narratives that drive real impact. Whether you're presenting to executives, collaborating with technical teams or communicating findings across departments, ACTED offers a practical roadmap for turning insights into initiatives that matter.

The ACTED framework

ACTED provides a repeatable, end-to-end template for storytelling with data. From focusing on who you're speaking to (Audience) through to how you present and follow up (Delivery), it integrates the human, contextual and technical elements needed to ensure your data story sparks action, not just understanding, ensuring that you:

- **Tailor** your narrative to the right people (Audience)
- **Frame** insights so they're relevant and meaningful (Context)
- **Build** a compelling storyline from problem to resolution (Tale)
- **Design** clear, impactful visuals that reinforce your key messages (Envision)
- **Present** the story in a way that drives decisions (Delivery)

By following this holistic approach, you ensure your analysis doesn't languish in a report or dashboard but sparks tangible action aligned with strategic goals.

Understanding your audience is the cornerstone of effective data storytelling. It involves identifying who you are speaking to, their roles, levels of data literacy and key concerns. A data story that captivates executives may fall flat with frontline managers who

Figure 12.1   The ACTED framework for communication of data insights

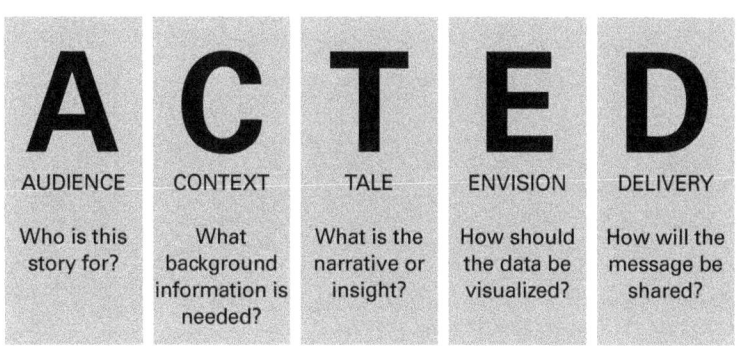

AUDIENCE	CONTEXT	TALE	ENVISION	DELIVERY
Who is this story for?	What background information is needed?	What is the narrative or insight?	How should the data be visualized?	How will the message be shared?

need operational details. Similarly, a highly technical explanation can alienate a non-technical team. By tailoring your message to meet the specific needs of your stakeholders, you ensure they see the value in your insights and remain engaged with your narrative.

Context provides the essential background that makes data meaningful. Numbers alone can feel abstract or disconnected; context bridges this gap by explaining why the findings matter. For example, is a sales decline due to a broader market shift, or is employee turnover linked to poor management practices? Context situates data within real-world challenges and opportunities, grounding your insights in trends, objectives or organizational priorities to foster a deeper understanding.

A compelling data story relies on a structured narrative arc, guiding the audience from a clearly defined problem, through insightful discoveries, to actionable resolutions. People are more likely to remember stories than isolated facts, as stories engage both logical and emotional faculties. By crafting a tale that connects the issue to a clear solution, you not only inform your audience but also resonate with them, driving engagement and buy-in for the next steps.

Visuals are the scaffolding of a great data story, turning raw information into clear and digestible insights. Designing effective visuals, such as charts, dashboards or infographics, ensures your story remains focused and impactful. Poorly designed visuals, full of clutter or confusion, can undermine even the best-crafted narrative. By highlighting key trends, patterns and outliers, visuals bring clarity and precision, allowing your audience to grasp the main points quickly and confidently.

The delivery of your data story is the final step where insights transition into action. Whether through presentations, dashboards or interactive sessions, your method of delivery must align with the audience and the message. Choosing the right format, tone and pacing can determine whether stakeholders act on your recommendations or overlook them entirely. Thoughtful delivery ensures your audience not only understands your analysis but also feels motivated to adopt the solutions or explore the insights further.

While ACTED is presented as a sequence, Audience first, then Context and so on, it's more of an iterative cycle. You might start with Audience, but as you flesh out your Tale or design visuals, you may revisit who your audience truly is or refine the context if new information emerges. Each step enriches the others, creating a feedback loop that enhances clarity and impact. Indeed, in some cases, you might be told how the message needs to be delivered up front, before any analysis!

For example, if, during the Tale stage, you realize certain details would be irrelevant to a key decision-maker, you might circle back to Audience to adjust the depth or complexity of your narrative. Similarly, if new insights appear while designing visuals (Envision), you could revise the Tale or even the Context to incorporate updated data.

Knowing your audience

Imagine standing before an eager audience, about to reveal a data-driven solution that could transform a project or solve a longstanding problem. Yet the impact of your message hinges on one critical factor: knowing who you're speaking to and what they care about. In data storytelling, a one-size-fits-all approach rarely works.

Decision-makers, frontline managers and technical experts each have different priorities and levels of data familiarity. Unless you tailor your message to these unique viewpoints, your story can drift between underexplaining key points for some and overloading details for others.

This section introduces the concept of audience profiling, the foundation of effective data storytelling. By defining who your stakeholders are, their technical competence and what drives them, you'll be better equipped to shape your narrative and ensure your insights resonate. Whether you're presenting to executives who focus on high-level strategy or team leaders who need precise, tactical steps, customizing your story to fit their goals and preferences can make the difference between 'That's interesting' and 'Let's implement this right away'.

Building an audience persona

A well-crafted data story begins with a clear understanding of your audience. Audience personas, a concept borrowed from marketing and user experience design, help you identify the characteristics of your stakeholders and tailor your message accordingly. While personas can be highly detailed, covering personal motivations and communication preferences, a simplified approach can still be highly effective and easier to implement.

Without a persona, your communication risks being too complex or overly simplistic, losing the audience's engagement or failing to drive action. A basic persona helps you stay grounded in the audience's needs and expectations, ensuring your story resonates and remains relevant.

To create a useful persona, start by identifying the key challenges your audience faces. For instance, an HR Director might be concerned about rising turnover rates, while a Marketing VP may focus on improving lead conversion. Understanding their goals is equally important – a CFO might prioritize cost reduction, while an Operations Manager could be focused on increasing efficiency.

Next, consider their level of data literacy and technical expertise. Some stakeholders may prefer detailed methodology or statistical terms, while others might respond better to simple visuals and plain-language summaries. Role and seniority also play a part in shaping your message. Senior executives often look for strategic takeaways, middle managers might need operational details and individual contributors may require actionable instructions or dashboards to guide their tasks. Lastly, focus on the specific questions they need answered, such as a Marketing VP asking, 'How can we optimize budget allocation to boost ROI by 20 per cent?'

By outlining these factors, you create a concise and practical reference point that shapes your data story. It helps you decide which metrics to emphasize, how complex your visuals should be and how deeply to delve into statistical or operational details. With a clear understanding of your audience, you can craft a message that informs, engages and drives meaningful action.

Audience data literacy

Data literacy – the ability to read, interpret and critically assess data – varies widely among stakeholders. Some individuals may be highly skilled with pivot tables, regression models or machine learning, while others might feel lost at the mention of standard deviation. To communicate effectively, it's helpful to group your audience into three broad levels of data literacy: novice, intermediate and expert.

Novices have minimal experience with data and prefer plain-language explanations supported by simple visuals like bar charts. They benefit from a focus on one or two key metrics rather than being overwhelmed by an entire dashboard. Intermediate users are comfortable interpreting charts and discussing trends, and they may appreciate additional details such as margins of error or sampling methods to validate conclusions. Experts, on the other hand, are familiar with advanced analytics and visualizations. They often value deeper explanations of algorithms, data modelling or statistical confidence levels.

To engage audiences across these levels, start with a simple overview that offers clarity for novices while providing options to drill down into interactive dashboards or detailed appendices for advanced users. Even data-savvy stakeholders value clarity, so when introducing a statistic or technical term, include a brief explanation to ensure alignment and understanding.

By tailoring your communication to meet people where they are, you can deliver insights that resonate with novices without overwhelming them, while still providing the depth and rigour that more advanced audiences expect. This balanced approach ensures your message is both accessible and impactful.

Technical skill level

Understanding your audience's technical comfort level is necessary in shaping how much detail to include in your data story. A highly technical group may want to dive deep into methodologies, assumptions and intricacies, such as how regression analysis was performed or why certain variables were included. For such audiences, transparency and depth are essential. They value understanding the 'how' behind the insights.

On the other hand, non-technical audiences typically care more about the implications of your findings than the methods used to arrive at them. For example, instead of explaining the mechanics of a regression analysis, you might summarize: 'Employees who receive 10 or more hours of training per quarter report 15 per cent higher engagement.' Strip away unnecessary complexity and focus on the impact.

Be mindful of the terms you use. Words like 'variance' or 'confidence interval' might be clear to a technical team but confusing for a less experienced audience. When in doubt, simplify without losing accuracy. Remember, the aim is to make your story accessible while maintaining credibility.

Role and seniority

Stakeholders at different levels of an organization have varied priorities. Senior executives often focus on strategy, ROI and long-term implications. For them, concise, high-level takeaways are most effective. A visualization showing the potential financial impact of an initiative, paired with a brief narrative like, 'This training programme could save $500,000 annually by reducing turnover', speaks directly to their concerns.

Frontline managers or technical teams, in contrast, may require operational details to guide their day-to-day decisions. For instance, instead of broad outcomes, they may need insights into specific actions, such as how to allocate training hours or address engagement gaps in certain teams. For these groups, more granular data and actionable recommendations are crucial.

Always consider the stakeholder's role when crafting your story. A data-driven marketing strategy might include detailed customer segmentation for a marketing team but focus solely on projected ROI for the executive team. Tailoring your story ensures relevance and increases the likelihood of engagement and action.

Managing bias

Human biases inevitably influence how data is received and interpreted. Recognizing these tendencies allows you to address them proactively, ensuring your story resonates while maintaining credibility and clarity. Confirmation bias, for instance, leads audiences to favour insights that align with their existing beliefs. If your findings challenge those beliefs, it's essential to present them alongside compelling evidence and context. For example, if engagement scores unexpectedly increased during remote work, you might say, 'While we expected engagement scores to drop during remote work, the data shows a 10 per cent increase, possibly due to flexible schedules and reduced commute stress.'

Anchoring bias highlights the power of first impressions, making it crucial to start your presentation with the most compelling insight. Opening with a key finding, such as 'Departments investing in employee training have a 20 per cent lower turnover rate', grabs attention and anchors the discussion around a critical takeaway. Similarly, the recency effect causes audiences to focus on the most recent data, so it's important to provide a balanced narrative that shows trends over time. For example, you might say, 'Engagement scores improved by 8 per cent last quarter, continuing a steady rise over the past year' to highlight a broader context rather than over-emphasizing the latest figures.

Understanding these psychological tendencies helps you frame your data story in ways that connect with your audience while reducing the risk of misinterpretation or resistance. While there are many other types of bias and psychological factors to navigate, simply being aware of their existence is a strong starting point. This awareness enables you to plan your communication more effectively, ensuring your insights are both impactful and credible.

Building connection and trust

The ultimate goal of understanding your audience is to foster trust and connection. When stakeholders feel that you've tailored your message to their needs, they're more likely to engage with the data and act on your recommendations.

For readers seeking a deeper dive into the topic and a tactile approach, the Data Storytelling Cards (find these on the website accompanying this book) offer a practical way to explore audience characteristics in greater depth. These cards can help you think critically about who you're presenting to and how to adjust your message accordingly. By building a detailed audience profile, tailoring your message, and addressing potential biases, you ensure that your data story resonates and drives action. Remember, the audience isn't just a recipient of your story, they're an integral part of it. Understanding them is the first step toward creating a story that matters.

Context: framing the story

Numbers on their own can feel lifeless, disconnected from the day-to-day realities your audience faces. Context is what breathes life into those numbers, turning them into insights that resonate and prompt action. Whether you're explaining a 10 per cent drop in revenue or a 15 per cent rise in employee engagement, the backdrop against which these figures appear, like economic conditions, organizational goals or even seasonal fluctuations, helps people understand *why* the data matters and *what* should be done about it.

If Audience is about *who* you're talking to, then Context is about *why* they should care. Done right, context gives each data point a purpose, ensuring the story you tell isn't just a collection of facts, but a narrative tied to real-world stakes. This section explores the different types of context and the techniques you can use to anchor your insights in a way that's both credible and compelling.

Types of context

Data storytelling doesn't occur in isolation; the environment, both internal and external, plays a crucial role in shaping how findings should be interpreted. The context you apply to your analysis depends on your stakeholders' priorities and the nature of your insights. There are several important types of context to keep in mind, and your stakeholders are at the top of that list.

Stakeholder context is critical to aligning your message with the goals and concerns of your audience. For instance, an HR Director focused on turnover might interpret a 5 per cent drop in engagement as a pressing issue, while a CFO might view the same data through the lens of cost implications. Tailoring the context ensures your insights resonate.

Strategic context ties data insights to broader organizational goals, reinforcing their importance. If the company's goal is to expand market share by 10 per cent, framing your analysis – such as identifying a new customer demographic – as a contributor to that objective makes your findings more relevant.

Social trends, such as the shift to remote work, can influence metrics like engagement or productivity. Including societal context adds depth and nuance to your analysis. Similarly, historical context provides a backdrop for current trends. For example, linking a decline in morale to last year's company reorganization connects past events to present issues.

Temporal and seasonal factors often explain data patterns, such as high retail sales in December due to Christmas shopping or summer spikes in hospitality metrics. Recognizing these influences ensures your analysis is realistic and accurate.

Economic conditions, like inflation or market growth, also impact performance metrics. For example, rising material costs during inflation might explain shrinking profit margins, offering clarity to trends that might otherwise seem puzzling.

Policy and regulatory context is essential when laws or compliance requirements affect data. For instance, labour laws encouraging retention might skew turnover metrics, making it vital to highlight these influences for accurate interpretation.

Geographical context reveals location-specific challenges, such as higher shipping costs due to remote distribution centres, while operational context links data trends to internal factors like workflow changes or resource constraints. A dip in manufacturing output, for instance, might coincide with maintenance downtime.

Market and competitor contexts provide benchmarks and comparative insights. A drop in sales might be tied to a competitor's new product launch, or a 5 per cent decline in market share might seem less alarming if competitors are experiencing an 8 per cent dip.

The key to using context effectively is selecting the elements that best illuminate your data. Focus on those that address stakeholders' immediate challenges or strategic goals, blending additional contexts as needed to enrich the story. This targeted approach ensures your analysis is both relevant and impactful.

Anchoring context

Even the strongest data can lose its impact if it lacks clear relevance to the audience or organizational goals. Grounding your insights in meaningful context ensures they resonate and drive action. One effective approach is identifying the deeper *why* behind the data. Techniques like the 5 Whys can help you dig beneath surface trends to uncover root causes. For instance, if employee engagement is down 10 per cent, asking successive *why* questions might reveal that the issue stems from a recent policy change, poor management or a cultural shift. Similarly, linking insights to SMART (Specific, Measurable, Achievable, Relevant, Time-bound) questions established earlier in the process ensures the data aligns with well-defined objectives. For example, if a primary goal is to reduce costs by 15 per cent, demonstrate how your findings support that target.

Another key strategy is connecting insights directly to organizational goals. Tie your data to KPIs that matter most to decision-makers, such as how improved engagement can enhance retention or how better lead conversion contributes to revenue growth. Referencing strategic documents like the annual business plan or company-wide initiatives adds an additional layer of credibility and relevance, showing that your insights are not isolated but part of a larger narrative.

When people see why an insight matters within their specific context, they are more likely to internalize and act on it. For example, a finance manager who understands how operational metrics directly contribute to cost reductions is more inclined to support and advocate for your recommendations. By rooting your data in the *why* and aligning it with organizational priorities, you ensure your message not only informs but also inspires.

Providing context is more than a single step in storytelling; it's an ongoing process that ensures your audience not only understands the insights but also feels compelled to act on them. Here's a structured approach to embedding context into your data narrative effectively.

1. Start with the 'why'

You will recall the SMART framework we used earlier in the book to help us come up with what was important to focus on before diving into the numbers. This helps us establish why the analysis matters to your audience. Connecting the data to a meaningful purpose or business objective helps ground your story and captures your audience's attention.

For example, if your story focuses on employee engagement scores, don't just present the numbers. Instead, frame the story with its potential implications: 'Engaged employees are 20 per cent more productive and less likely to leave the organization. Today, we'll explore how engagement has shifted over the past six months and what it means for our retention strategy.'

Starting with the *why* ensures your audience sees the relevance of your analysis from the outset, aligning their focus with the insights you're about to present.

2. Explain data credibility

Context loses its impact without trust in the underlying data. Establishing the credibility and reliability of your data is essential to convincing your audience that the insights are worth their consideration.

For example: 'This data comes from our annual employee engagement survey, which had an 85 per cent response rate across all departments.'

Highlighting the source, methodology and robustness of the data gives your audience confidence in its accuracy. Avoid overwhelming them with technical jargon; focus instead on what makes the data reliable and relevant.

3. Link to past trends or knowledge

Data storytelling is most effective when it builds on what your audience already knows. Linking new insights to past trends or discussions provides continuity and deepens understanding.

For instance: 'In last quarter's meeting, we discussed how increasing training hours was starting to improve engagement scores. Today, we'll look at how those changes have continued to impact team performance.'

By connecting your story to previous insights or events, you create a narrative thread that helps your audience see the bigger picture. This continuity not only reinforces trust in your analysis but also ensures your insights feel like part of a cohesive strategy.

4. Focus on immediate relevance

While long-term implications are important, your audience often needs to know how insights apply to their immediate concerns. Highlighting the here-and-now impact of your data ensures your story feels actionable.

For example: 'Addressing the disengagement in this department could save us $150,000 in turnover costs over the next six months.'

Providing immediate relevance ensures your audience feels the urgency and practicality of your insights. It also primes them to focus on the steps they can take right away. A well-contextualized data story combines these elements seamlessly. Start by answering why your audience should care, back it up with credible data and tie the insights to previous discussions or trends. Finally, emphasize the immediate relevance of the findings. By embedding this step-by-step approach into your data narrative, you not only ensure your insights are understood but also make them compelling, actionable and aligned with your audience's goals. Context transforms raw data into a story that drives decisions and inspires action.

Tale: crafting the narrative

Every great story, whether in a book, a film or a conversation, follows a narrative arc. This arc, a structured journey from beginning to end, is what captures our attention, makes us care and leaves us with something to think about. The same holds true in data story-telling. Without a narrative, even the most compelling insights can feel disjointed and forgettable. A clear narrative arc transforms raw data into a meaningful journey, guiding your audience from understanding a problem to embracing a solution.

Humans are wired to understand and retain stories far better than isolated facts or figures. A list of statistics may explain what's happening, but a well-told story illuminates why it matters and what should be done. Consider this: if you're presented with data showing a decline in employee engagement, you might shrug it off. But if the data is framed as a story about departments struggling with low morale, leading to high turnover and rising costs, the issue suddenly feels urgent and personal. Stories not only engage the mind but also connect with emotions, making them far more persuasive and memorable.

A well-structured narrative in data storytelling is like a road-map. It provides a clear path for your audience, showing them where the journey begins (the problem), the key stops along the way (the insights) and the ultimate destination (the resolution). Without this structure, your audience risks getting lost in the details or missing the bigger picture. A story creates clarity, focus and purpose, key ingredients for turning data into action.

In this section, we'll explore how to build that roadmap, ensuring your insights are not just heard but remembered and acted upon. A compelling data story is built on three fundamental pillars: the problem, the insight and the resolution. Each pillar serves a distinct purpose, guiding your audience through the narrative and ensuring they stay engaged, understand the message and know what action to take. Let's explore each pillar and how it forms the foundation of a successful data narrative.

1. Problem: setting the stage

Every story begins with a problem, a challenge or opportunity that captures the audience's attention and sets the context for why the data matters. Defining the problem upfront helps ground your audience, giving them a reason to care about what follows. It also establishes relevance by connecting the data to real-world stakes.

For instance, imagine presenting to a leadership team: 'Turnover rates have increased by 15 per cent over the past year, costing the company $500,000 annually.'

This simple statement does more than just share a statistic; it highlights a tangible issue with significant financial implications. Starting with the problem immediately focuses your audience's attention and makes it clear why the analysis matters. When framing the problem, it's essential to ensure clarity and alignment with the audience's priorities. Is this problem something they are directly responsible for addressing? Does it relate to their organizational goals? By defining the issue in terms they find relevant, you set the stage for the rest of your story.

2. Insight: illuminating the path

The insight is the heart of your data narrative. It's where the data moves beyond numbers and charts to reveal a deeper understanding of the problem. Insights bridge the gap between raw data and actionable knowledge, providing clarity and focus on what's driving the issue or opportunity.

For example, after presenting the turnover problem, you might share this key finding: 'Engagement scores in departments with higher turnover are 20 per cent lower than the company average, suggesting a strong link between disengagement and turnover.'

This insight connects two pieces of data – turnover rates and engagement scores – to offer a deeper explanation of what's happening and why. It allows your audience to see the story unfolding, leading them naturally to ask, 'What should we do about this?'

Crafting insights requires not only interpreting the data but also articulating them in a way that resonates with your audience. Avoid overloading your audience with too many findings; instead, focus on the most critical insights that advance your story and answer the audience's key questions.

3. Resolution: driving action

Every great story needs an ending, and in data storytelling, the resolution is the call to action. This is where you propose clear, actionable steps based on the insights you've uncovered. A strong resolution aligns recommendations with organizational goals and provides a roadmap for addressing the problem or seizing the opportunity.

Continuing the turnover example, you might propose: 'Implementing targeted training programmes in low-engagement departments could improve retention and save $250,000 annually.'

This recommendation not only addresses the problem but also ties it back to the audience's priorities, retention and cost savings. By emphasizing the potential impact, you make it clear why action is necessary and how it aligns with the organization's goals. The resolution should leave no ambiguity about what needs to happen next. Whether it's launching an initiative, allocating resources or changing a process, the resolution should empower your audience to take action confidently.

Leveraging contrast

Using contrast effectively in storytelling can elevate your data narrative, making it more engaging and impactful. By juxtaposing opposing elements, what was versus what could be, or high-performing segments against low-performing ones, you create a clear and compelling frame that highlights the significance of your findings. This approach not only draws attention to key insights but also underscores their relevance, encouraging your audience to think critically about potential actions or outcomes.

One common technique is leveraging before-and-after comparisons to demonstrate change or progress. For instance, you might highlight, 'Team A had a 20 per cent attrition rate before adopting a new training regimen. Six months later, that rate dropped to 10 per cent.' This approach works because it showcases tangible improvement or decline, making the impact of a strategy or the consequences of inaction undeniable. The audience can clearly see the value of a decision, reinforcing the importance of data-driven interventions.

Another effective use of contrast is juxtaposing challenges and opportunities. Consider this example: 'While the retail division struggles with a 5 per cent drop in foot traffic, our e-commerce channel grew by 12 per cent thanks to targeted social media ads.' Such comparisons not only reveal trade-offs or disparities but also encourage strategic reflection. They push the audience to consider shifts in investment, resource allocation or priorities to address challenges while capitalizing on emerging opportunities.

By weaving contrast into your narrative, you make differences and potential courses of action more vivid, answering the crucial 'so what?' of your data story. This approach ensures that your audience stays engaged, understands the stakes and is motivated to explore actionable solutions. Contrast is a powerful tool for turning raw data into a narrative that resonates deeply and drives decision-making.

Storyboarding your tale

Storyboarding is a helpful step in planning your data narrative, much like a film director sketches out each scene to create a seamless storyline. By visualizing the flow of your narrative, you can ensure that each data point, insight and recommendation fits cohesively within the problem → insight → resolution structure. Storyboarding provides clarity and coherence, helping to eliminate confusion or redundancy while ensuring your message resonates with your audience.

To begin, map out the key scenes of your story. Start by identifying the main points: the problem you're addressing, the key data or insight that reveals the root causes and the proposed resolution or actionable recommendations. Arrange these components in a logical order, using sticky notes, a whiteboard or a digital diagram to sketch the flow. This method not only helps you organize your thoughts but also makes it easy to rearrange elements as needed to enhance the story's impact.

Figure 12.2   A storyboard example

PROBLEM	INSIGHT	RESOLUTION
Employee engagement scores dropped by 15% over the past year, particularly in teams with fewer training opportunities.	Analysis shows teams with fewer than 10 training hours per quarter had a 25% higher attrition rate.	Launch targeted training programmes for teams with low engagement and training hours.
KEY METRIC Engagement Score (–15%)	**CORRELATION/CAUSE** Training → Retention	**RECOMMENDED ACTION** Provide 10+ hours of training per quarter for all teams.
IMPACT *Higher attrition and reduced productivity.*	**DATA FINDINGS** *Engagement directly linked to training opportunities.*	**KPI** *Track engagement scores post-intervention.*

For example, imagine your story revolves around improving employee engagement (see Figure 12.2). In the 'Problem' section, you might highlight a 15 per cent drop in engagement scores over the past year. In the 'Insight' section, show data indicating that engagement dipped most significantly in teams with fewer training opportunities. Finally, in the 'Resolution' section, recommend targeted training programmes, supported by visuals like a bar chart comparing training hours to engagement scores.

Envision: creating impactful visuals

Visuals are the foundation of a compelling data story. They bridge the gap between raw data and understanding, transforming complex information into accessible insights that inspire action. In the Envision step of the ACTED framework, the focus is on designing visuals that enhance the narrative, making the story clear, engaging and actionable.

Effective data visualization goes beyond simply displaying data; it clarifies meaning, emphasizes priorities and supports decision-making. A well-designed visual achieves three critical objectives: it communicates the core message immediately without the need for extensive explanation, highlights key trends, patterns or outliers, and directs attention to actionable insights, helping the audience understand what matters and why it matters.

As a very simple example, let's look at two ways to visualize which department has the lowest engagement scores.

Table 12.1 Engagement score table

Department	Engagement score (%)
Sales	75
Marketing	60
IT	80
HR	55
Finance	65

In Table 12.1, each department is listed with its corresponding engagement score. While this does give us the details we are interested in, it requires the reader to scan each row and manually compare the numbers of each department to determine which has the lowest score.

By contrast, if we use the same data but visualize it as a bar chart (Figure 12.3), we can more readily identify the answer to our question and sort that HR is the worst performer.

Figure 12.3   Engagement score chart

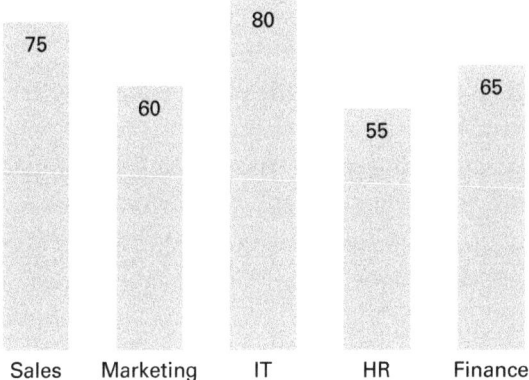

This is not to say that tables don't have their place, but in this example, all the same data is visible in both representations, and the bar chart is more visually appealing and accessible to a wider audience.

Defining the core message

Before creating any visual, ask yourself a question: what do you want your audience to remember after seeing this visual? The answer to this question becomes the core message that should guide the design and purpose of your visualization. Without a clear message, a visual risks confusing your audience or weakening the impact of your story.

Each visual should have a distinct purpose within your narrative, aligning with the story's goals to reinforce the central insights you're communicating. For instance, when illustrating a problem, a line graph showing a steady decline in employee engagement over the past year vividly highlights disengagement trends, making the issue undeniable. To support an insight, a scatter plot might reveal a strong positive correlation between training hours and employee retention, bridging the gap between data and decision-making. When highlighting a resolution, a side-by-side bar chart comparing current costs with projected savings from a new initiative can make the solution feel tangible and achievable.

By defining the core message first, you ensure your visuals remain focused, purposeful and impactful. This clarity transforms visuals into a powerful tool for communicating your narrative effectively and driving action.

To maximize their impact, visuals must align seamlessly with the narrative arc of your data story. Think of visuals as the chapters within your story: each one builds on the last, moving from problem to insight to resolution. This alignment keeps your audience engaged and guides them toward actionable outcomes. With this approach, your visuals not only support your story but also become an essential part of how your message is understood and remembered.

Picking the right charts

When choosing the right charts, simplicity is key. There is no single chart type that works universally for all situations. Instead, the best choice depends on the story you want to tell and the relationship or pattern you're trying to highlight. By focusing on clarity and functionality, you can ensure that your charts effectively communicate your message.

Line charts are a go-to choice for illustrating trends over time. If you need to show how metrics like monthly sales or engagement scores have changed, a line chart provides a clear, continuous picture. It allows your audience to easily identify patterns such as growth, decline or seasonality, keeping the focus on how things evolve.

For comparing categories or groups, bar charts are the most effective option. Whether you're showing departmental turnover rates or market share by region, bar charts make it simple to identify which categories are leading or lagging. Both vertical and horizontal bars can be used depending on the space and the type of comparison being made.

Sometimes, a single chart may not capture the full story. In such cases, combining simple charts can help. For example, placing a bar chart that displays monthly costs alongside a line chart showing monthly revenue can reveal relationships between the two. This pairing might highlight how changes in expenses directly influence profit margins, making complex insights more accessible.

It's also important to avoid chart junk, unnecessary elements that add visual clutter without adding value. Features like 3D effects, excessive gridlines and distracting animations often confuse more than they clarify. A clean, minimal design ensures that the data remains the focal point. By keeping your charts straightforward, you guide your audience to the insights that matter most.

When more detail is needed, consider showing your charts in a logical sequence rather than cramming too much into a single visualization. This approach keeps each chart focused while still building a comprehensive story. Ultimately, the goal is to keep things simple and intuitive, so your audience can quickly grasp the key takeaways.

Storyboarding the visual flow

Building on the narrative structure (Problem → Insight → Resolution), storyboarding visuals (Figure 12.2) provides a framework for crafting a seamless and logical data story. By pre-planning the sequence of charts, you ensure that your visuals align with your message, stay simple and guide your audience toward the desired conclusions without confusion or distraction.

Start by identifying the essential visuals for each part of the story, sticking to straightforward chart types like line charts, bar charts or combinations of these. For the Problem, you might use a line chart to illustrate the 15 per cent drop in employee engagement scores over the past year, showing the progression clearly and highlighting the magnitude of the issue. In the Insight section, a grouped bar chart can compare teams with high versus low training hours, emphasizing the correlation between training and engagement. Finally, in the Resolution, a side-by-side bar chart can illustrate the projected improvement in engagement scores post-intervention, demonstrating how targeted training could yield tangible results.

Keep your charts focused and uncluttered to ensure clarity. For example, when showing engagement trends over time in a line chart, avoid adding excessive data points or gridlines that might distract from the main message. Similarly, in a grouped bar chart comparing teams, use distinct yet subtle colours to differentiate groups without overwhelming the audience. The goal is to make the key insights immediately apparent.

Transitions between visuals are critical for maintaining flow and keeping your audience engaged. Use brief, descriptive captions or headers to connect the story. For instance, after the line chart in the Problem section, include a caption like, 'This decline prompts a deeper look into what's causing disengagement.' Then, transition to the Insight bar chart with, 'Teams with fewer training hours reveal a significant gap in engagement.'

By adhering to a storyboard and using simple, impactful visuals, you ensure your data story is not only easy to follow but also compelling. This approach highlights the insights while avoiding unnecessary complexity, allowing your audience to focus on the actions needed to address the problem and implement solutions effectively.

Focusing attention: designing for impact

Visuals are most effective when they guide the audience's attention to the critical insights. In the Envision stage, the focus is on designing visuals that prioritize clarity and impact while removing distractions. By directing attention to what matters most, visuals become powerful tools for enhancing understanding and driving action.

Each visual in your story should have a clear focal point that communicates its key message. Emphasize critical data points or trends using techniques like bold colours or larger elements. For instance, in a line graph tracking employee turnover, a contrasting colour can highlight a sudden spike, making the insight stand out immediately. Annotations, such as labels, arrows or callouts, can further draw attention to essential areas. For example, labelling a peak in engagement scores with a note about a new training programme provides valuable context and directs focus to a significant moment.

Simplicity is equally important in making visuals impactful. Complex datasets should be transformed into clean, digestible visuals, such as replacing a dense spreadsheet with a focused bar chart that highlights the most relevant metrics. By simplifying the presentation, you ensure the audience can quickly grasp the takeaway and engage with the insights confidently.

Figure 12.4 Keeping visual simple and directing attention

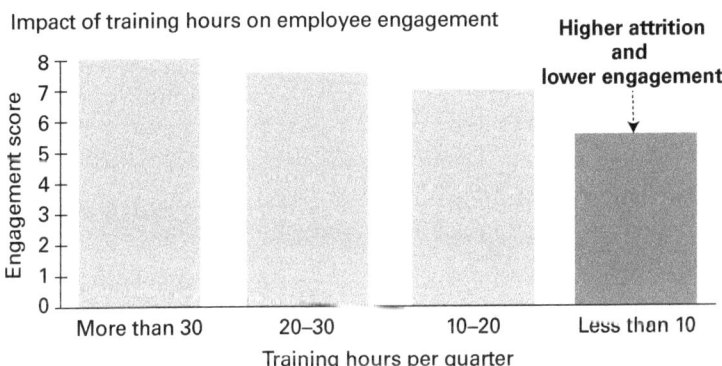

The field of data visualization can go very deep; however, to get a sense of how you can use charts in a simple yet effective way, see the example in the final section.

Delivery: presenting the story

No matter how profound your insights or how polished your visuals, the final step, *Delivery*, is where your data story truly succeeds or falls flat. This is the point at which your analysis leaps off the page and into the decision-making process, influencing minds and inspiring action. In the Delivery stage of ACTED, you'll consider how format, tone and timing converge to maximize engagement and solidify your narrative's impact.

Choosing the right format for delivery

Just as you tailor the depth of analysis and style of visuals to your audience, selecting the right delivery method is equally important. The format you choose should resonate with the audience's preferences and fit the context of the situation, whether it's a high-stakes presentation to senior leadership or an informal discussion with cross-functional peers.

In-person presentations are ideal for real-time interaction, allowing you to gather immediate feedback and align strategically. Executives often value a concise slide deck that highlights key points, while data-savvy audiences may prefer a deeper dive into the details. Presenting in person also enables you to adjust your tone, pacing and level of detail based on the room's reactions.

Reports work well for detailed analyses or as a permanent record of findings. A well-structured PDF or printed document allows stakeholders to revisit metrics and commentary at their convenience, making it a reliable tool for reference and decision-making.

Interactive dashboards are particularly valuable when your audience needs regular updates or the ability to explore data independently. Platforms like Power BI or Tableau provide dynamic views of metrics, making dashboards a useful choice for teams that monitor KPIs daily or weekly, such as frontline managers tracking operational performance.

Infographics are an excellent choice for less technical or broader audiences, distilling complex insights into visually engaging and easy-to-understand formats. They emphasize key findings and high-level takeaways without overwhelming the reader, making them ideal for communicating with a diverse group.

For example, a CFO might prefer a concise, data-rich report for auditing purposes, while a Marketing VP could benefit from an interactive dashboard to explore campaign performance. Selecting one or two formats that align with your audience's workflows and decision cycles ensures that your findings are accessible, actionable and impactful.

Structuring the delivery

The effectiveness of your delivery relies heavily on how well you organize your story. A disorganized presentation can obscure your insights, while a well-structured approach draws the audience in and keeps them engaged through to your final recommendation.

Begin with a compelling hook to grab attention immediately. Highlight a striking data point or pose a question that underscores the significance and urgency of the topic. For example, 'Over the past quarter, we lost $300,000 in preventable costs: what caused it and how do we fix it?' Starting this way ensures the audience understands the importance of the discussion right from the outset.

As you move through your presentation, build momentum by logically guiding the audience through the problem, key insights and resolution. Use visuals and narrative flow to illustrate each main point, ensuring that charts or tables tie directly back to the overarching data story. This logical progression maintains clarity and helps the audience stay focused on the core message.

Conclude with actionable recommendations that clearly articulate the 'so what' of your insights. Summarize your findings in practical steps, specifying who should take action, what they need to do and by when. For example, you might end with, 'By implementing a targeted training programme, we can cut turnover by 15 per cent in the next six months, saving nearly $250,000.' A strong call to action leaves no ambiguity about the next steps.

In time-constrained situations, such as a five-minute executive briefing, focus on the most critical data points and prioritize the top one or two recommendations. Respecting your audience's time and attention span ensures your message is both impactful and well-received. A structured, concise delivery keeps your insights sharp, actionable and memorable.

Engaging the audience

Delivery is often a two-way street. While you're presenting your data story, your audience is forming questions, drawing their own connections and preparing to challenge or accept your proposals. By proactively engaging them, you foster dialogue and commitment to the insights.

In live settings, whether in person or virtual, consider embedding a quick poll or quiz. Ask, 'Which factor do you think most influences turnover?' before you reveal your data. This approach not only piques curiosity but also surfaces preconceived notions you can address.

Think through likely objections or questions your audience may have. If you're recommending more training spend, be prepared to show how it fits into the budget or how it compares to competitor benchmarks. Demonstrating foresight in addressing concerns boosts credibility and trust.

Keep an eye on nonverbal cues (furrowed brows, nods or confusion) to gauge how well the message is landing. Encourage real-time clarifications: 'Does this chart make sense? Any questions on this metric before we move on?'

One helpful tool is this simple matrix (see Table 12.2) matching delivery methods (e.g. dashboards, PDFs, presentations, infographics) against audience types (executives, frontline managers, technical teams, cross-functional stakeholders).

The matrix clarifies not just *how* but *why* you might choose one format over another, ensuring each audience gets what they need in a form they'll find accessible and actionable.

Effective data storytelling culminates in a presentation, however brief or elaborate, that compels your audience to see your insights not merely as interesting facts but as actionable imperatives. By

Table 12.2 Delivery methods matrix

Audience/format	PDF report	Interactive dashboard	Slide deck	Infographic
Executives	Good for detailed metrics they can read on their own time	Possibly too granular unless high-level summary provided	Effective for concise strategic sessions	Useful for high-level overview; easy to distribute
Frontline managers	Could be overwhelming if too long	Excellent for daily metrics; fosters quick decisions	Works if it includes direct action steps	Might lack the operational detail they need
Technical teams	Highly valued for in-depth analysis, especially with methodology included	Great if they want to explore data slices themselves	Could be effective for walk-throughs	Might be too simplified unless designed for clarity
Cross-functional	Good reference tool, but may not drive immediate engagement	Helps individuals from diverse areas see relevant metrics at once	Can unite people around a shared vision if data is well organized	Quick snapshot for alignment if minimal detail is required

choosing the right format, structuring the narrative for clarity and maintaining active engagement, you elevate your data from abstract charts to a potent driver of organizational change.

No matter how superb your analysis, if stakeholders remain uninspired or uncertain about the next steps, your data story has not fulfilled its potential. Delivery is the stage where your hard work truly shines, turning insight into action in the minds of those who can make the greatest impact.

Telling a compelling story

As we close this chapter on data storytelling, it's crucial to recognize that insights alone are rarely enough to drive meaningful change. The ACTED framework – Audience, Context, Tale, Envision and Delivery – provides a comprehensive structure to ensure your data narrative not only informs but also resonates, engages and compels action. Each stage, from understanding your audience to delivering your story, builds upon the other, creating a seamless flow that transforms raw data into a catalyst for decision-making.

By tailoring your message to your audience's needs and aligning your insights with their goals, you lay the foundation for a story that truly matters. Context ensures your findings are grounded in real-world relevance, bridging the gap between abstract numbers and practical implications. Through a structured narrative arc, you guide your audience through the problem, highlight the key insights and present actionable resolutions. Clear and focused visuals amplify the story, allowing your audience to grasp the significance of your insights quickly and confidently. Finally, delivering your story effectively ensures it doesn't just sit on a page or a dashboard but inspires real action.

This chapter has offered tools and techniques to move beyond merely presenting data to crafting stories that drive outcomes. However, the true power of ACTED lies in its iterative nature. Data storytelling is rarely a linear journey; it requires reflection, adaptation and refinement as new insights emerge and audience needs evolve. This dynamic process ensures your narratives stay relevant and impactful, no matter the context.

In the next chapter, we'll bring the ACTED framework to life through a practical application using our HR example. You'll see how each stage of ACTED can be applied to a real-world scenario, bridging theory with practice. By the end of this book, you'll not only understand the framework but also feel confident in your ability to tell data stories that inspire change and make a lasting impact.

Let's turn the page and put ACTED into action.

Example

Up to this point, you've learned how to craft a compelling data story through the ACTED framework: understand your Audience, establish Context, build a cohesive Tale, design clear visuals in the Envision stage and, finally, Deliver insights so they ignite action. Now, we'll walk through a practical application of ACTED using the same HR scenario carried throughout the book, especially the Software Development team findings from Chapter 11. You'll see each stage of ACTED come to life, transforming raw analysis into a persuasive story that sparks change. As a reminder, here is a quick recap of where we are:

- **Software Development turnover**: 15 per cent (vs. 9 per cent company-wide), with a Q2 spike from 10 per cent up to 18 per cent.

- **Key finding** (Chapter 11): Hypothesis testing showed a strong link between low training hours (<6 per quarter) and low engagement in the Software Development team. Increasing training was predicted to raise engagement and potentially reduce turnover.

The HR analytics team believes a targeted training initiative will mitigate Software Development's turnover problem. However, leadership won't act on raw data alone – they need a clear, compelling story. That's where ACTED comes in.

Audience: Tailoring your message

The first step is identifying whom you're telling the story to, what challenges they face, what goals they have and how they want data presented. Below are personas for the key stakeholders involved in addressing Software Development turnover:

Persona 1: CFO

1 Key challenges

- o Under pressure to reduce costs and optimize budget allocations.

- o Concerned about the company's bottom line and ROI on any new initiative (like training).

2 Goals

- o Achieve tangible cost savings, e.g. reducing the annual $500K expense associated with Software Development turnover.

- o Maintain or improve financial health by ensuring departments stay within budget.

3 Data literacy

- o Comfortable with interpreting ROI calculations, summary metrics and high-level financial charts.

- o Prefers clear, numeric insights but doesn't need raw statistical detail.

4 Technical level

- o Satisfied with a high-level overview of the analysis (no deep-dive into regression coefficients).

- o Appreciates a breakdown of financial projections, not detailed Python scripts or model equations.

5 Role and seniority

o Executive-level influence, signs off on budget changes.

o Expects concise, strategic takeaways over operational minutiae.

6 Key questions

o 'Will investing more in training truly justify the cost?'

o 'How soon can we expect to see a return on this investment?'

Persona 2: Software Development Manager

1 Key challenges

o Facing department morale issues after a Q2 reorganization.

o Struggling to retain both junior and senior developers in a tight labour market.

2 Goals

o Reduce Software Development turnover from 15 per cent down to company-wide levels (target ~10 per cent).

o Improve team productivity and morale, especially for new hires (<1 year tenure).

3 Data literacy

o Intermediate understanding: can interpret engagement metrics and turnover trends.

o Prefers straightforward visuals (bar or line charts) highlighting the Software Development team's progress.

4 Technical level

o Doesn't need code-level detail but wants clear evidence of what interventions work.

o Appreciates some operational breakdown (like training hours vs. engagement scores).

5 **Role and seniority**

o Departmental leadership in charge of day-to-day decisions.

- o Influence over team culture and immediate operational changes.

6 **Key questions**

- o 'What can we do right now to prevent another Q2 turnover spike?'
- o 'How do we implement the training pilot without disrupting deadlines?'

Persona 3: HR Director

1 **Key challenges**

- o Overseeing the entire organization's employee engagement and retention strategies.
- o Needs to balance fairness across departments while complying with data governance rules.

2 Goals

- o Align Software Development interventions with broader HR objectives, such as lowering overall turnover from 9 per cent to 7 per cent.
- o Ensure compliance with company policies, labour laws and data privacy regulations.

3 Data literacy

- o Comfortable reading summary tables and key statistics (like p-values).
- o Prefers some detail on data credibility and methodology, e.g. survey response rates.

4 Technical level

- o Interested in how data was collected and validated (methodology).
- o Doesn't require code-level detail but wants to know enough to answer internal audits and policy queries.

5 Role and seniority

- o Senior HR leadership, shapes culture and policies organization-wide.
- o Strategic influence to scale successful pilot programmes across multiple departments.

6 Key questions

- o 'Does this training programme align with our overall HR initiatives (e.g. leadership development)?'
- o 'What policies or approvals are needed to roll this out consistently across teams?'

Why this matters: By clarifying these personas, you'll adapt tone, detail and visual style in your final presentation or report. For the CFO, highlight cost and ROI; for the Software Development Manager, show immediate operational tactics; for the HR Director, stress strategic alignment and policy compliance.

Context: explaining why it matters

- **Stakeholder context**
  - o **Software Development Manager:** Recalls a Q2 reorganization leading to an 18 per cent turnover spike, with morale dips among now hires.
  - o **CFO:** Recognizes $500K lost annually to Software Development turnover (from cost estimates in previous chapters).
  - o **HR Director:** Must maintain fairness and sees Software Development's issues as a microcosm of broader culture challenges.
- **Strategic context**
  - o **Reduce Software Development team turnover** from 15 per cent to 10 per cent by year-end.
  - o **Lower overall turnover** (currently 9 per cent) to 7 per cent.

o Fulfill the company's goal of being a 'Top Employer' by enhancing career development.

- **Why now?**

  o **Budget timing:** The CFO needs final decisions on next-quarter funding.

  o **Hiring surge:** An influx of junior Software Development hires are in their first year, a known risk window for early exits.

  o **Data credibility:** Analysis is based on a robust 12-month dataset with an 85 per cent engagement survey response rate.

By rooting your story in relevant contexts – organizational goals, immediate Software Development pain points and ongoing budget cycles – the entire leadership team grasps *why* Software Development's turnover isn't just an isolated HR problem but a strategic priority.

Tale: building the narrative arc

Problem: turnover and low engagement

You begin your story with the problem:

'Software Development turnover spiked to 18 per cent in Q2 compared to the company average of 9 per cent. This translates to roughly $500K in lost productivity and recruiting costs.'

This statement speaks directly to financial concerns for the CFO, operational concerns for the Software Development Manager and overall retention goals for the HR Director.

Insight: under-training leads to higher exit risk

Move to the insight:

'From our hypothesis testing (Chapter 11), Software Development employees who log fewer than 6 training hours a quarter have engagement scores 8 points lower than those who complete 6+ hours. This correlates with a significantly higher turnover likelihood – our p-value of 0.02 confirms it's not by chance.'

Here, you connect data-based evidence to real departmental struggles. A short explanation of p-values might suffice for the HR Director's methodology interest, while the CFO just needs to see the strong relationship with measurable impact.

Resolution: targeted training initiative

Conclude with the resolution:

'Implement a structured training programme ensuring each Software Development member gets at least 8 hours of training per quarter. We project engagement could climb back to the mid-70s, cutting turnover from 15 per cent to near 10 per cent in six months, saving $250K.'

Contrast helps reinforce why action is crucial:

'Prior to Q2's reorg, Software Development turnover was around 10 per cent. After employees lost consistent training budgets, turnover soared to 18 per cent. Restoring and boosting training hours can recapture those lower turnover levels.'

Envision: creating impactful visuals

- **Highlight the problem**
  - **Line chart:** Software Development turnover each quarter vs. the company average. Emphasize Q2's 18 per cent peak.
  - **Bar chart:** Compare average engagement by quarter, showing Software Development's drop from 71 to 63.
- **Depict the insight**
  - **Grouped bar chart:** Engagement scores among Software Development employees with <6 vs. >6 training hours.
  - **Option:** Add a small annotation explaining p=0.02 (for those curious about methodology) near the chart.
- **Demonstrate the resolution**
  - Side-by-side bar chart:

- **Left bar:** 15 per cent turnover 'Before' the initiative.

- **Right bar:** Projected 10 per cent turnover 'After' with a $250K cost-saving arrow or label.

- **Keep visuals clear and minimal**

  o Use bold colour for key metrics (turnover spikes, training thresholds).

  o Provide short captions, e.g. 'Low Training Hours = Lower Engagement, p=0.02.'

  o Eliminate chart junk so the main takeaway is unmistakable.

Delivery: presenting for impact

- **Choosing the right format**

  o **CFO:** Present a succinct slide deck with cost analyses, plus a short PDF or Excel summary for offline review.

  o **Software Development Manager:** A live conversation or in-person presentation focusing on immediate action steps.

  o **HR Director:** Include a brief infographic tying the training programme to broader HR initiatives (like fostering a 'Top Employer' brand).

- **Structuring the discussion**

  o **Hook:** 'In Q2, Software Development's turnover cost us $300K – here's how we can fix it.'

  o **Build:** Show the line chart of turnover, then the bar chart of engagement vs. training hours.

  o **Conclude:** 'We propose an 8-hour-per-quarter training pilot to save $250K in six months and stabilize Software Development's morale.'

- **Engaging the audience**

  o **Q&A:** Invite the CFO to evaluate the cost-benefit analysis. Ask the Software Development Manager about logistical concerns or scheduling.

- o **Quick poll:** 'How many training hours do you believe are feasible per quarter?'
- o **Address objections:** If the CFO worries about budget, display a short ROI table. If the HR Director worries about fairness, describe how you can replicate the training model across other departments.

You foster a two-way dialogue that cements everyone's commitment to the solution.

Putting it all together

By following each stage of ACTED – Audience, Context, Tale, Envision and Delivery – you craft a data story that clearly outlines why Software Development turnover is a pressing issue, what the data reveals about training hours and engagement, how to solve it and which steps are needed to implement your solution:

- **Audience**
  - o CFO: Cost savings and ROI.
  - o Software Development Manager: Immediate solutions for retention.
  - o HR Director: Organizational alignment and compliance.
- **Context**
  - o Ties back to strategic goals (lower turnover, better engagement).
  - o Q2 reorg fiasco triggered morale decline.
  - o $500K annual cost if unaddressed.
- **Tale**
  - o **Problem:** High Software Development turnover, $500K cost.
  - o **Insight:** Under 6 training hours correlates with an 8-point engagement drop.
  - o **Resolution:** 8-hour/quarter training initiative targeting a 5 per cent turnover reduction (saving $250K).

- **Envision**
  - o Use a line chart (turnover trend), grouped bar chart (training vs. engagement) or side-by-side bar chart (projected turnover drop).
  - o Keep visuals uncluttered, highlight key numbers.
- **Delivery**
  - o Short, high-impact presentation for CFO and Software Development Manager.
  - o Infographic or one-pager for HR Director.
  - o Interactive Q&A fosters buy-in and real-time feedback.

Outcome: The Software Development Manager adopts the training programme, the CFO endorses the budget and the HR Director integrates the initiative into a broader engagement strategy. Over time, Software Development turnover declines from 15 per cent towards 10 per cent, fulfilling the organization's strategic objective and demonstrating how well-crafted data stories drive tangible results.

Exercise

Choose a business challenge or question relevant to your organization (e.g. 'How can we improve customer retention?' or 'Why are sales declining in specific regions?'). Use the ACTED framework to craft a compelling data story that drives actionable insights.

1 Audience

- o Identify who your audience is (e.g. executives, team leaders or external stakeholders).
- o Define what they care about most and what decisions they need to make based on your story.

2 **Context**

o Frame the business problem clearly.

o Include relevant background information or trends that make the issue pressing and relatable.

3 **Tale**

o Develop a narrative arc for your data story.

o Highlight key findings, insights and connections in a way that logically leads to your recommendation.

4 **Envision**

o Select or sketch a visualization (e.g. bar chart, line graph or infographic) to communicate the most critical part of your story.

o Ensure the visual aligns with your audience's needs and enhances clarity.

5 **Delivery**

o Write or present a short summary of your data story.

o Focus on delivering clear, actionable recommendations that align with your audience's goals.

Reflection questions:

● How did applying the ACTED framework help refine your data story?

● What adjustments did you make based on your audience's needs or the context of the problem?

● What feedback would you seek to improve the story further?

Summary points

1 **Personas bring clarity**
Detailing each stakeholder's challenges, goals, data literacy and technical needs ensures you address the right points and format your content for maximum impact.

2 **Context fuels urgency**
Linking Software Development turnover to strategic goals and immediate budget considerations shows why action is necessary now.

3 **Narrative arc (tale) creates cohesion**
Problem → Insight → Resolution organizes your analysis into a digestible, memorable story.

4 **Visuals amplify the message**
Clean, targeted charts highlight the correlation between training hours and engagement, reinforcing the recommended solution.

5 **Delivery seals the deal**
Presenting in the right format, allowing for Q&A and tailoring discussions to each persona's concerns lock in stakeholder buy-in and operational follow-through.

This practical example underscores how the ACTED framework isn't just theory, it's a roadmap for making your data insights resonate, whether you're addressing a critical turnover challenge in a Software Development team or any other data-driven initiative across your organization.

NEXT STEPS

Congratulations on getting this far! You've taken the crucial first steps on your journey to mastering data interpretation. By now, you've built a strong foundation in understanding the key principles, frameworks and techniques covered in this book. If you followed along with the examples and exercises in each chapter, you've seen how the theory can be applied to specific scenarios, gaining a practical understanding of how to approach data-driven challenges.

But as with any skill, the true test lies in real-world application. Theory provides the blueprint, but practice in complex, imperfect environments sharpens your ability to uncover insights, make decisions and drive meaningful change. The data you'll encounter in your organization may be messy, incomplete or overwhelming. You may face challenges like stakeholder scepticism, limited resources or unclear objectives. These are the realities of working with data – and the opportunities to make an impact.

Where to go from here

To help bridge the gap between theory and practice, visit the website for this book at www.howtointerpretdata.com. Here you'll find additional resources, including:

- **Real-world scenarios:** Work through curated, industry-specific case studies to refine your skills.
- **Interactive exercises:** Test your understanding of key concepts with hands-on challenges that mimic real-world data situations.
- **Downloadable tools and templates:** Access ready-to-use tools to simplify frameworks like SPOT, BRICE and ACTED and apply them to your own projects.

Becoming a data-driven leader

The most effective data practitioners aren't just those who can crunch numbers, they're the ones who can ask the right questions, communicate insights clearly and align data analysis with organizational goals. Keep in mind:

- **Practise the frameworks:** Use the SPOT, BRICE and ACTED frameworks in your day-to-day work. The more you use them, the more intuitive and impactful they'll become.

- **Adapt to context:** Tailor the principles in this book to fit your unique challenges. Every organization and dataset is different, and the ability to adapt is key.

- **Engage stakeholders:** Collaborate with colleagues, involve decision-makers, and use data to build consensus and drive action.

- **Stay curious:** Data interpretation is a constantly evolving field. Commit to continuous learning, whether through courses, books or staying up to date with industry trends.

Final thought

Your data journey doesn't end here, it's just beginning. The next steps you take will define how you apply the skills you've gained to solve real-world problems, elevate your career and make a lasting impact. The tools are in your hands; now it's up to you to use them.

Good luck on your journey, and thank you for letting this book be a part of it.

EU Representative (GPSR)

Authorised Rep Compliance Ltd, Ground Floor, 71 Lower Baggot Street, Dublin, D02 P593, Ireland

www.arccompliance.com

www.ingramcontent.com/pod-product-compliance
Lightning Source LLC
Chambersburg PA
CBHW060354040525
26135CB00031B/311